Gertrude Hoyt Memorial

M. Bieri

How to Boost Your Return on Management

How to Boost Your Return on Management

Edward C. Schleh
President, Schleh Associates, Inc.
Palo Alto, California

McGraw-Hill Book Company
New York   St. Louis   San Francisco   Auckland
Bogotá   Hamburg   Johannesburg   London
Madrid   Mexico   Montreal   New Delhi
Panama   Paris   São Paulo   Singapore
Sydney   Tokyo   Toronto

80709

Library of Congress Cataloging in Publication Data

Schleh, Edward C.
  How to boost your return on management.

  Includes index.
  1. Industrial management. I. Title.
HD31.S3329 1984   658   83-5452
ISBN 0-07-055306-8

1234567890BKP/BKP89876543

ISBN 0-07-055306-8

The editors for this book were William A. Sabin and Diane M. Krumrey,
the designer was Naomi Auerbach, and the production supervisor
was Teresa F. Leaden. It was set in Primer by ComCom.

Printed and bound by The Book Press.

Contents

ABOUT THE AUTHOR

Edward C. Schleh is a widely recognized management authority. His name has become synonymous with the concept of "results management," which he has developed and applied successfully in a wide range of industries over the past thirty years. The National Society for the Advancement of Management has awarded him the prestigious Frederick Taylor Award in recognition of his outstanding contribution to the management field. Mr. Schleh is the author of several management bestsellers, including *Management by Results* and *The Management Tactician*. His pioneering work appears in major business periodicals and in translation around the world. He lectures frequently to top management groups in the United States and abroad and is a past director of the Council for International Progress in Management.

Preface

All executives and managers feel that they can analyze management problems effectively. The disappointingly low increase in productivity suggests that this is not true. In my experience their basic approach is often wrong. Their prime focus is on return on investment. Instead, it should be on securing the maximum return or value from their management talent. It is the source of all productivity.

In my previous book, *The Management Tactician,* I tried to present principles executives should use to manage well. In this book I am trying to show by examples how to analyze and solve any management problem and apply these principles effectively to increase the return on management.

The cases used have been selected from several hundred in my company's files. For over twenty-five years we have analyzed and solved management problems in a wide diversity of operations. In most assignments we have helped the client carry through to make sure the recommendations worked in practice. For this book I have selected cases that I felt everyone could relate to. The analytical approach has been applied effectively in other kinds of operations, too, like banking, insurance, and nonprofit and government organizations. For obvious reasons the cases have been camouflaged to avoid identification.

Since the cases go into some depth, each presents specific

solutions to segments of an overall management problem. Their main value, however, is to serve as illustrations of the analytical approach described in Chapter 1. With the overall management perspective developed, the reader may then apply the analytical approach to different problems.

I am indebted to the many friends, clients, and associates who have helped me develop this analytical approach over the years. I am especially indebted to Robert T. Davis of the Graduate School of Business of Stanford University, John Walsh of the Graduate School of Business of Washington University, Alan Ofner of Managing Change, Inc., and Dwight Tudor of the Dwight Tudor Co. Overall, my former associate, Edwin R. Hodges of Business Analysis International, has made substantial contributions in reviewing the manuscript. My wife, Myra, has been a helpful critic all through its development. My editor, William Sabin, has been patiently helpful in getting the manuscript into a viable book. Although many people have had an impact on my thinking, I alone must bear the responsibility for any errors or weaknesses of the book.

Edward C. Schleh

How to Boost
Your Return
on Management

CHAPTER 1
Motivating for Greater Management Return

It is a continuing challenge to executives to effectively meet competition—local, national, or international. To do this they must maximize the return from the human, physical, and financial resources under their control. Attempts have been made to pinpoint direction by use of return on investment (ROI) or return on assets (ROA). These have been effective but limited in their impact. The real key to accomplishment is ROM—return on management (ROM). This return-on-management effort throughout the organization depends far less on strategic decision making than it does on the management style established by the executive and the meticulous attention given to the application of that style. The best management style should motivate management people toward maximum return. Do not all management styles encourage maximum return? On the contrary, management styles unintentionally often discourage return because management principles are misapplied.

WELL-APPLIED PRINCIPLES CAN
INCREASE RETURN

1. Do Not Reward People for
What They Do

Many management systems reward people for what they do; this approach leads to lower return from management. Instead, people should be rewarded for what they accomplish (for the results they get) *not* for what they do; these are not the same thing. A major reason for this emphasis is that in modern complex enterprises, results are usually achieved by cooperation with others; they are not usually achieved by one person individually. Putting the emphasis on what individuals do often pushes them away from cooperation and compromise, and so away from results. To encourage cooperation, therefore, rewards should be based on results that are achieved in collaboration with others. Such an approach rewards for cooperative results not just for individual results.

2. The Total Is Not Equal to the
Sum of the Specialized Parts

With the rapid increase in specialized knowledge a popular misconception has gained credence: If all specialized tasks are done well, greater accomplishment will result. This is not true; specialties are frequently in opposition to each other. Even in this specialized age, pushing each specialized part to its limit almost always results in less total productivity; the total result is reduced because the work accomplishment of some other specialists is reduced. The total is not the sum of the parts.

In management specialized contribution must be compromised in order to get maximum net accomplishment. Less specialized accomplishment of one type often means greater overall results if it then blends with the contribution of another specialist.

3. Productivity Depends on
Tactics, Not on Strategy

Executives often feel that their prime job is the formulation of strategy; through it they can make their greatest contribution to productivity. They assume that successful strategy will automatically get results—after executive decision everyone will carry through on the strategy as planned to the greater results expected. It does not work that way; contrary to popular wisdom, only tactics finally get results. Slavish adherence to strategic plans frequently results in less ROM because it is almost impossible to visualize all future productivity problems. Management tactics should be a primary executive concern in order to get maximum accomplishment—in most cases a greater concern than strategy. Tactics are not simply something to be delegated; they must be nurtured and followed up. A prime job of an executive is to make sure that the tactical management environment encourages maximum productivity in real life at all levels of the organization.

4. An Executive Should Be Primarily Concerned with ROM at the First Management Level

Overall management productivity depends on the productivity of the first level of management. It is commonly assumed that first-level results are a matter of delegation and should not be a personal concern of executives. They should not be concerned with these smaller details; they should focus on the big picture. On the contrary, first-level ROM is a matter of delegation to be sure, but it should still be the primary concern of executives. Executives should be actively involved in getting the kind of management environment that encourages maximum productivity down the line. All the policies, procedures, organization structures, and programs that they approve set this environment.

5. It Is Not the Primary Function of the Jobs Below to Carry Through on Executive Decisions

"Ours not to reason why—Ours but to do or die." Employees today, quite properly, do not accept this dictum. The philosophy that carrying through on executive decisions is the prime function down the line is activity-oriented, not results-oriented, and actually leads to less ROM. No results may be accomplished by the activity; local problems may interfere. In addition, a great flurry of activity gives the illusion of accomplishment and often leads to unrealistic complacency. It is much sounder to look at the function of jobs below as that of getting the results that executives need to accomplish. Every effort should be made to encourage people down the line to exercise their ingenuity and initiative to get results at their levels. No executive or staff miracle worker can visualize all the permutations of local problems.

6. It Is Not the Principal Job of Staff to Inform the Executives

Many executives visualize staff primarily as their communication link. It is stifling to the organization to assume that the primary purpose of staff is to report deficiencies of those below and to keep executives informed so that they can make decisions. Staff then becomes a gestapo instead of a valued aid to the organization. Record functions are especially subject to this misconception.

Staff expertise is much more effective in the organization if its primary function is viewed as that of helping executives accomplish results by helping people below get more results. In other words, staff should be the helper of everyone below in achieving maximum productivity—right through the bottom level. This philosophy encourages maximum ROM to be achieved from their expertise.

MANAGEMENT CAN CAUSE NEGATIVE PRESSURES

How can these and other management principles be applied to develop a management style that encourages top ROM; how can misapplication of them be prevented? We need a new way of looking at management. Popular wisdom has suggested that executives should delegate the responsibility for action and concentrate on the big decisions. On the contrary, our work with several hundred organizations, large and small, points up the need for executives to be personally involved in the management climate for productivity that exists throughout the organization.

A pattern has emerged; a new management approach is called for.

The basis for this new management approach is the simple proposition that executives should make worthwhile accomplishment advantageous to all management people. All the pressures on a management person should be synchronized toward results expected; executive attention should be focused so that these pressures do not push away from these results. A prime job of every executive is to establish a holistic management approach that balances all the various pressures on people at every level to maximize their productivity. There are pressures in every job pushing the person in the direction of accomplishment, but unfortunately there are also many pressures pushing against accomplishment and preventing achievement. The kind of misapplication of management principles discussed earlier develops one type of negative pressure. Various programs, policies, and procedures may cause these negative pressures.

Some programs that produce negative pressures were probably well-intentioned and usually helpful at the time they were instituted, but they may not fit the productivity requirements today. Management environments are always changing, so pressures that were sound yesterday may be negative today. In addition, some programs exert a positive influence on one result but at the same time exert negative pressures on other results, creating imbalance. In effect, they decrease overall ROM.

WHAT KIND OF PRESSURES AFFECT ROM?

Policy and Procedure Pressures

Executives may set policies and establish their inevitable concomitant procedures that act very restrictively on people down the line. Productivity is affected because the action that gets results is usually at the bottom of the organization. The policies may have been thought of as controls rather than as ways to guide and stimulate people and may, therefore, affect productivity negatively. Procedures, in turn, are usually ways to force uniformity, and uniformity is rarely a good way to encourage high productivity in all jobs; the day-to-day requirements of jobs are different. Further, procedures frequently go beyond policy intent and thus retard accomplishment by control never envisioned by the policymakers. Executives must curb this overkill.

Organization Pressures

A number of pressures antagonistic to ROM can occur because of organization design. For example, decision making may be centralized because an executive wants to control the operation. But the effect is to restrict initiative below, adding a negative pressure on people below, thereby holding back productivity.

There may be so much specialization of work that there are too many people in every action. This phenomenon has been a common problem in recent years because of the greater and greater breakdown of various disciplines. It seems logical to a thinking executive to have the expert do the work, whatever it may be. In most cases, though, all expert work must be compromised with that of other experts in order to get a result; an executive must balance off their impact. Otherwise the experts exert pressure against maximum results. Overspecialization is a potent force working against ROM in many organizations.

The span of management may be too broad, creating managerial time pressure; as a consequence, managers may not have time to cover their responsibilities. Many executives have not recognized that the most important point where this affects results is at the bottom; management literature has mistakenly overemphasized executive span. Many first-level supervisors are beyond their span of management, however, so that they cannot be maximally productive. Since the practical result of the work of higher management usually has to show up at the bottom levels, overall ROM is reduced.

There could also be a deadening effect of too narrow a span, one over one or one over two. In these cases extra management people become too involved in the work below and restrict initiative there. Many people become involved in every problem. In addition, extra levels of management result. Since each level adds about 25 percent to communication problems, it is more difficult to get decisions made and sound action instigated. ROM is affected.

Information Pressures

The whole record and information system can restrict initiative at any level. Sometimes the information system allows current records to go to higher managers in detailed form, and those managers, in turn, get into too much detailed managing. In some cases there is an overemphasis on cost data, not on productivity data, creating a pressure toward imbalance. At other times restrictive accounting practices result in misdirection of people below; budget and cost emphasis may not be consistent with management direction and, therefore, acts as a restraint on accomplishment.

Reward System Pressures

An executive may have approved a company reward system that is not geared to spur people to higher productivity. These systems may focus on activity, rewarding people for doing things not for getting results; this type of reward pushes people away from productivity. Reward systems may focus on the wrong results, or on a single area of results, and, therefore, not encourage balanced results and a net higher ROM. One example of this is the almost chronic overemphasis on the short range.

A major problem with reward systems is that they often do not reward for results coming from group action. In any modern organization it is rare that individual action gets maximum accomplishment in any part of the operation; most results come from the combined work of several people. When executives base rewards on individual accomplishment, the rewards are often antagonistic to cooperative results. True accomplishment has to be measured in terms of these joint results.

As a consequence of these negative pressures, executives are lucky if they get 50 percent value out of the abilities of their people. It is the job of management to eliminate as many of these negative pressures as possible and to create a management environment that increases positive pressures so that each management person is encouraged toward maximum ROM. A responsibility of top priority for every executive is the establishment and maintenance of a management climate that maximizes these positive pressures throughout the organization.

MAKE NEGATIVE
PRESSURES POSITIVE

How can an executive decrease the negative pressures on people that prevent higher ROM and increase the positive pressures on them? There is an analytical discipline available to any manager by which positions can be analyzed in order to make all the pressures positive and thereby increase ROM.

What Is the Loss or Gain?

The first step in analyzing a management problem is to ask, What is the loss to the organization by the present method of operation, or what is the potential gain being missed. If possible, the losses or gains should be measured in terms of the final results of the institution; in most companies these measurements would be in dollars. The loss should not be defined simply as a problem such as lack of morale (what is the effect?), inefficiency (too broad), excessive number of people (what evidence do you have?), or poor organization (how do you know?).

The loss should not be defined as a violation of management principles; good management is constantly compromising management principles to get specific results. A rigid devotion to a management principle decreases ROM. Even an apparent imbalance in emphasis is not a loss unless you can show that there is a lack of accomplishment in a measurable result. Many losses are made up of a number of subparts, so they must be analyzed down to each subloss in order to be susceptible to analysis and improvement.

What Caused the Loss?

The next step is to determine what directly caused the loss. There is always something that triggered off the loss; it could be something physical (like a switch or machine chatter), or it could be the action of a person. It might even be several items that interact with each other. Each of these factors must be ferreted out. It is too simple to say that a loss is caused by lack of communication, lack of cooperation, or lack of credibility. In our experience, such a conclusion rarely helps in solving a management problem. Some machine, some piece of paper, or some person's act was a trigger that led to the loss.

Which Management Action Caused the Cause?

It is interesting that every cause which triggers a loss or prevents a gain originated somewhere in some management action; it did not come out of the blue. That management action was originally well-intentioned and probably aimed at a particular problem. The problem may no longer exist, however; or else, while the action is positive for one result, it adds a negative pressure against the accomplishment of another result and so is retarding ROM. The management action may have been the establishment of a policy or a procedure; it may have been a specific management decision; it may have been a requirement to report in detail; etc.

Why the Action?

Even though there was usually a logical reason for these management actions, the action may not have corrected the problem. It may have considered only one facet of the problem, or it may not have considered other problems affected by the action. It is important to find out why the action was instituted; what the rationale was behind it; whether the reason was adequate; and whether it covered the whole problem. This part of the analysis almost always leads to violations of management principles. A good understanding of management principles is, therefore, helpful in understanding the impact of the action.

Solve the Problem

If the first four steps of the analytical process have been well carried out, the fifth step, arriving at a solution, is almost automatic. The old saying that a problem well-analyzed is a problem solved is pretty well true of management problems. This total analytical process is the basis for achieving higher ROM.

DEVELOP A MANAGEMENT STYLE
FOR MAXIMUM ROM

In summary, the management style is the basis for higher ROM. Management principles that guide the operation must be carefully reviewed to make sure they are realistic when applied to live management problems, their application leads to positive pressures on people in the organization, and they encourage people to work toward higher ROM.

The key to getting higher ROM (and therefore higher productivity in general) is to recognize that people react to the pressures of their management environment. Creative management strives to reduce the negative pressures and increase those that are positive. Executives can, therefore, make a major contribution to management results by creating a management climate that encourages positive pressures throughout the organization.

The best way to analyze the effect of these pressures is the four-step process:

1. Isolate the loss or potential gain.

2. Determine the cause of the loss.

3. Decide which management action occasioned the cause—the source of the pressure.

4. Find out why management took that action.

This approach to solving the ROM problem is the core that runs through this book; the various facets of this approach are developed in the succeeding chapters. It is the basis for maximizing the return from the management people in any kind of operation. It allows executives to productively utilize the immense reservoir of untapped ability that lies dormant in every management group.

2 Making a Total Company Profitable

If a once-profitable company declines and gets into the red, it is extremely difficult to stay this negative momentum and make the company profitable again. Executives too frequently look for *the* thing that caused the decline. On the contrary, the decline is usually attributable to a number of different influences, all contributing in some way to a lack of ROM.

An example is a company that manufactured and sold condensers to original-equipment manufacturers. Because of its special technical know-how, the firm had been very profitable for a number of years. Then for some unapparent reason profits started to go down, and a recession finally forced the company into losses. The firm had a manufacturing department, an R&D department, and a sales and marketing department. It was critical that they quickly analyze the reasons for the decline, correct them, and turn the company back into the profit column.

GET COSTS UNDER CONTROL
AT EVERY LEVEL

The first step in analyzing this company's ROM was to look at the causes of increased costs. It became clear that even though a budget system had been in effect, the management system had not been exerting adequate pressure toward cost control.

Make Pay Reward Cost Control

An underlying problem was that the management reward systems did not emphasize the control of costs. For example, the executive and management bonus plan was ostensibly based on profit, presumably including an emphasis on costs. All the upper-management people shared in the profit bonus based on their base salaries, following a compensation plan approved by the board of directors. Over a period of years profits had fluctuated somewhat but had been consistently good. Essentially, the same bonus had been paid year after year, creating the illusion that all management people had done a good job. As a consequence corrective action on cost problems had not been pushed; since bonuses were good, there seemed no urgency. As is frequently true in profitable companies, each person felt that the good profit was attributable, at least in part, to the fine way he or she had been operating. The system actually encouraged everyone to become complacent; it did not encourage a vigorous attack on cost problems.

In addition, the bonus plan developed a tendency to resist change. The problem was exemplified by the general superintendent, who had received the same bonus year after year while achieving little cost improvement. He had put a great deal of emphasis on employee relations and very little on improving efficiency; it was easier than rocking the boat with incisive action on costs.

It is common practice in many companies to set up executive bonuses based on company profit because the firm is engaged in trying to make a profit. The theory is that all are encouraged to cooperate for maximum profit. But more often than not, profit bonuses detract from pushing contribution toward better profit. They reward the poor contributors about as well as the top contributors and tend to overemphasize the short term.

The cost problem had been accentuated by the account managers, who were the people who called on the firm's customers. Because they wanted their customers to be properly serviced, they had no compunction about going right into the plant to correct any kind of problem relating to their customers; this action disrupted supervisory control and increased manufacturing costs. But the account managers were not accountable for their effect on plant costs.

Another contributing factor to the cost problem, strangely enough, had been the standard cost system used for pricing. Why had a standard cost system increased costs? When costs had gone up, prices had gone along with them, and for a time the firm's high product quality had allowed it to sell to its customers even at these higher prices. The bonus system had continued to pay good bonuses and had not, therefore, forced a review of costs. The recession and then competition had developed customer resistance to the high prices, however. Prices had to be lowered with the consequence of lower profit and, finally, losses.

The first step that the chief executive had to take to correct the cost problem was to change the whole management objective system and set realistic objectives for every key position, in light of the balanced results that should have been expected from each job. Control of costs was included. He then proposed a new bonus plan to the board that was tied to these new objectives, rather than simply to profit as such. The plan encouraged balanced results in each job, including costs. As a case in point, the objectives and the bonus plan of the general superintendent were changed, placing special emphasis on improving his cost per unit. Shortly after the change, he came back from the plant and commented that he couldn't stand the "idle time" he saw because "it affects my bonus." It was now advantageous for him to control costs.

Prevent Participation from Reducing Productivity

In addition to the reward system, the management mode of operation of the firm itself had led to poorer productivity. Executives had been oversold on participation as the key to good management; they felt that if all were involved, all would be committed and great accomplishments would result. As a consequence the firm had been operating by a series of committees. Although many of the committees had been originally designed to inform, people were often using them to discuss their individual problems. They had thereby subtly dumped their individual responsibilities onto the committees.

The company had thought the committee approach was the way to get cooperation toward results—since all were in on a problem and agreed on a solution, they would, of course, all help to make it work. But participation had not necessarily made everyone feel committed to the result. Our American culture is not the same as the Japanese culture, where the group system encourages people to feel committed to what the group agrees to. Participation can be helpful, but not as an end in itself, and not as the total mode of operation. It can be helpful as an aid to other management techniques.

The consequence of participation in this company was that people had found committees an easy way to duck accountability. For example, the plant manager had had a daily planning committee in the plant, where everybody in a key plant position had talked about the problems of the day. Since daily problems tended to be departmental and sectional problems, they brought up their own problems for the plant group to solve. No one in the group had been individually accountable for the consequences of any decisions made; members of the group had not felt accountable for accomplishment because the problems were not in their specific responsibility. In addition, the people who should have been accountable had felt that they were off the hook because "everyone had agreed." These meetings had also taken a great deal of time of the key people.

It had been apparent that some control was needed to compensate for the lack of accountability. The firm had put in a "bad egg" report to focus attention on plant problems. This report highlighted any problem that had occurred during the day, by the place and supervisor where it had occurred. However, any supervisor who could have explained away the reason for the problem was in the clear—and they had all become alibi experts. But these explanations had not stimulated incisive corrective action. Explanations had served as a substitute for accountability.

The committee problems had started with the executive committee, which met four to six hours twice a month. Here, too, many responsibilities of individual executives had been discussed. All executives had become involved in each problem discussed so that it had been hard to get individual executives to push forward on their own individual objectives. The president had felt that all should be in on a problem because, as executives, they should all be interested in all company problems. One effect of this approach had been that the inexperts on the executive committee had often unduly influenced detail that was beyond their expertise. For example, the controller might have had the same influence on a customer sales problem as had the vice president in charge of sales; the vice president in charge of sales might have had the same influence on an industrial relations problem as had the vice president of industrial relations, even though the former knew little about plant operations.

The president then changed the system so that the executive committee only met two hours a month. In addition, they discussed only those items that were broad company problems and were not in the individual responsibility of one member alone. To further force responsibility to a person, whenever the executive committee discussed a broad problem in someone's particular area, that individual would act as chairperson. For example, if the overall subject of budget policy was discussed, the controller was chairperson during that time. The controller, therefore, became much more accountable for the effect of any budget changes that were made. It was up to the controller to lead the discussion to workable solutions.

Fifteen regular committees in the plant were disbanded. The "bad egg" report was also eliminated. In their place the vice president of manufacturing established a system of objectives for all supervisory personnel that made them firmly accountable for cost achievement in their areas. Appraisals were then based on these objectives.

Make Managers of the First Level

These steps only set the basic framework for cost control. Another problem occurred because the foremen had not been supervising their crews; they had not been incisive on their crew's problems. Why not? They had been encouraged to get help from higher management whenever they thought it would have been helpful. In the process both foremen and superintendents had been relieved of responsibility for a problem if they had asked for help on it; the foremen had, therefore, ducked accountability by simply passing it upward. They had been conduits for problems rather than problem solvers. The committee form of operation had encouraged this approach.

This mode of operation was then changed so that foremen were made accountable for costs in their own sections, whether they received advice or not. The rule of *completed delegated work* was put into effect; foremen and superintendents were made accountable for the results expected of them, whether or not they got help from anyone else. Getting help did not relieve people of accountability.

Many executives fall into this trap of taking managers off the hook for accomplishment of results if they have the foresight to ask somebody else for advice on the problem. It seems logical that you cannot hold people accountable for poor results if they follow the advice of a superior. This practice leads to a weakened management group. Managers should be accountable for results no matter whose advice they follow.

An added factor still prevented good first-level supervision. The union contract forbade the foremen from working on any part of the hourly jobs. This common contract setup made it difficult for foremen to train and supervise their crews. They could not show the operators how to do a job or correct an error. The vice president of industrial relations had to work out an agreement with the union that allowed foremen to work 20 percent of the time on the hourly work under them. They could then spend the time necessary to train, supervise, and direct their people—to make them effective. Only then could they be fully effective first-level supervisors. That is the prime job of first-level supervisors, to train and direct the work of their people.

But even with these changes the foremen were still not in a position to fully affect their operation. Why? Many of them were beyond their span of management. They were trying to supervise more than they could handle. They did not have time to adequately supervise all their people; lack of time prevented them from managing fully. The fact that they did not have time to do everything needed in supervision further fortified the idea that they should not be held accountable and, in addition, should ask someone else for advice.

The obvious solution was to reduce their span; the executive group had to approve the addition of more first-level foremen—increasing the indirect-to-direct ratio. Span of management is frequently a problem in companies, but at the bottom management level, not at the top as is suggested in management literature. Executives succumb to the tempting reduction of the indirect-to-direct ratio by cutting down on first-level supervision and, as a consequence, sow the seeds for lower productivity.

Maintenance Is the Foreman's Job

Another aspect of the cost problem was machine maintenance cost. This had been viewed by line supervision as essentially a problem of the maintenance department, not as the responsibility of the line foreman or superintendent. After all, the line managers did not supervise the maintenance people, and maintenance was not production work; therefore, it was the job of the maintenance foreman. This attitude had implied that the line foremen had not had to be concerned about costs due to maintenance problems: Maintenance problems had made up a discrete little bundle separate from production.

It is not sound to relieve the line of accountability for any part of its work simply because there is a staff group operating on a problem; the line should always be accountable, whether there is a staff group involved or not. Accordingly, accountability was changed in this plant so that the foremen were made accountable for total cost including maintenance cost; they could require maintenance whenever they wanted it.

Productivity Requires a
Continuous Work Flow

An additional loss had been occurring that was not corrected by these changes; it was caused by a fifteen-minute interval that had been established between the first and the second shifts. The interval had been set up to supposedly eliminate some of the confusion occurring at shift changes; presumably, the elimination of this confusion would help productivity. Contrary to expectations, however, the operation had lost momentum and, therefore, productivity during these intervals; the interval had reduced the flow of information between the two crews. The people going off the shift had wanted to go home immediately instead of waiting around in order to inform people on the next shift; the people coming on, in turn, had not wanted to come in early in order to receive information. This procedure had subtly further reduced the feeling of accountability of the foremen because they could more easily blame the other shift.

Shift schedules were then changed and the fifteen-minute interval was eliminated. Shifts were butt-ended, allowing a smooth transition from one shift to the other; each shift could pass on information to the next, and accountability was made firmer.

MAKE SERVICE DEPARTMENTS PRODUCE

The expertise of a number of service departments could have helped the operating people in the plant operate more effectively. The reason their advice had not been sought was that they had not been viewed primarily as assistants to the line.

Make Purchasing Fit Operations

The purchasing department was one department that had substantially affected plant productivity. The plant had frequently been delayed because the right materials were not on hand for particular orders. Purchasing had felt that its main job was to get materials at a good price. Production delays were the production department's problem. Purchasing had taken some responsibility for the inventory of major raw materials, but its feeling of responsibility for even that inventory was questionable. The prime weakness was that it had not felt accountable for any effect that it had on production such as shutdowns due to lack of materials; that was presumably the problem of the operating people.

This lack of balanced accountability is common in many purchasing departments. They are concerned about price because they control it directly; it is highly visible. They, therefore, get credit for it. They are not concerned about other indirect impacts they have on plant efficiency. These can often cost more than the savings made in prices.

The system was changed. Purchasing was still made accountable for the price of purchased materials; that was sound. In addition, however, it was made accountable for its effect on plant operation, including the losses due to shutdowns caused by materials, whether due to poor timing or to poor quality. Purchasing was then in tune with plant operations.

Maintenance Can Improve Line Productivity

The maintenance department had also affected machine shutdowns. In common with many other maintenance departments, this maintenance department had emphasized its maintenance cost but not its impact on machine running time or on line productivity. The primary purpose of maintenance should be to keep the machines running efficiently for the maximum period of time; it should not be primarily to maintain the machines as such or to correct maintenance problems after they occur. To be sure, the cost of downtime should be balanced off against the cost of maintenance work.

To better capitalize on maintenance experience, the emphasis in maintenance was broadened by the vice president of manufacturing; the maintenance department was made accountable for shutdown time due to lack of maintenance, as well as for maintenance cost. Since line supervisors were now accountable for total unit cost in their sections, including maintenance costs, they were willing to work cooperatively with maintenance people toward these same objectives.

Improve Methods

Utilizing the skills of the industrial engineering department to get better productivity posed another problem. The department had been broken down by specialty—one engineer was a specialist on conveyors, another on machines, another on handwork, and so on. Frequently, several industrial engineers had, therefore, been involved on an individual project. Each engineer worked only on his or her part and had not been tied in to the overall effect of the project on a particular production department. If the engineer's work seemed to show good analysis, he or she was commended even if no net improvement in productivity resulted. Industrial engineers were, therefore, not in tune with the objectives of line supervision.

For example, an industrial engineer had developed what appeared to be a good project on cost reduction by running some items on the big press. When the department ran these items on the big press, however, it had to take other items off the big press and run them on less efficient presses; the net improvement in plant efficiency was nil.

In addition, skilled industrial engineers had worked on many small projects. As a consequence they had not always focused on the big productivity problems of the line people. They were like any specialized staff, which tends to push items in its specialty even though they may not fit the total needs of the line operation.

The industrial engineering organization was changed so that each industrial engineer was made accountable for total cost improvement in a geographical area of the plant; each was then in tune with the foreman's responsibility. Industrial engineers became interested in training each foreman in simple methods work because it was apparent to them that they got more improvement in methods this way; they could stretch the application of their expertise. They could then devote more of their time to the big projects. Each was accountable for the balanced impact of all methods work, both positive and negative, on line results in a specific part of the plant.

Schedule for Manufacturing Productivity

Scheduling had been a special problem in getting high productivity because the firm was a job shop operation and there were many short runs. In addition, orders had been constantly changing during each month, so much so that the manager of planning and scheduling had only two outboxes on his desk: one was marked "rush" and the other, "superrush." Because of the many changes, planning and scheduling had naturally been deciding on the personnel needs of each plant department and section. The foremen had acquiesced because it was easier to go along and they were not accountable for cost anyway. The planning and scheduling department had, therefore, given them another way to duck accountability. However, the planning and scheduling department had not been accountable for cost either. It is a common error to let planners influence the work of the line but not be accountable for their impact.

As we mentioned earlier, foremen were now made accountable for their costs; they were, therefore, given the right to decide their personnel needs. Planning and scheduling was given the obligation of providing the personnel the foremen requested. In order to encourage planning and scheduling people to tie in well, the vice president of manufacturing made them accountable for plant cost too. They could help reduce costs by making the most effective schedules to get long runs by running similar products together and by providing the personnel that the foremen requested.

Quality Is a Line Problem

Quality control had posed an additional problem in getting high productivity. Naturally, the chief inspector had wanted to be sure that no product of poor quality ever got out to customers; this made sense because the firm had a reputation as a quality house. The president had stressed this. The chief inspector had, therefore, felt that it was his job to maintain that quality reputation emphasized by the president. To make sure of top quality, he had directed his inspectors to reject any product with a shadow of a blemish. This action forced costs higher than they should have been; customers had not required the high quality in most cases and the high standard had caused high waste.

The direct inspection work was then pulled out from under the chief inspector and placed directly under the line supervisors. Foremen and superintendents were made accountable for quality.

It is a common misconception of organization to assume that inspection should always be separate from line supervision. Many executives feel that manufacturing cannot be trusted with inspection. I have never seen an inspection department that produced quality; only line people produce quality. If foremen and superintendents are made accountable for the quality that they turn out, they are often quite capable of providing their own inspection.

The chief inspector was still retained, but he was made accountable for the quality of products sent out to customers and, in addition, for waste; he was, therefore, encouraged to balance optimum quality against waste. In addition, he was encouraged to train the inspectors and the foremen to make the best balanced decisions on quality. He, too, was now in tune with the line operation.

MAKE SALES PROFIT-MINDED

Profit had also been dragged down by the approach that the sales department had been encouraged to take. It may seem odd to look at the profit impact of salespeople, because you might think that the sales department's prime impact would be on volume. In this company, however, the sales department had an important impact on profit beyond just getting sales volume.

Make Sales Contribute to Profit

The starting point of the sales problem was the program the president had approved of narrowly assessing salespeople by volume alone; as a consequence, account managers had been given recognition only for their sales volume. It had, therefore, not been advantageous to them to push especially hard for profit, i.e., for margins for orders requiring special procedures, and for better timing of orders; it would have taken time away from selling volume. Since the firm was essentially a job shop and individual orders were often specials for a particular customer, every order could have had an effect on margins. In addition, each could have had a cost impact on the plant because of special variations in product or because of delivery dates that broke into schedules. The argument that had been given by the account executives was that "the customer required it."

The president then broadened the evaluation of the sales department to include all its impact on profit. As a consequence, the appraisals of account managers were changed so that their recognition was based on the profit from their accounts. All the extra cost of special production for their accounts as well as the extra cost of breaking into schedules for quick delivery was charged against them. It was now advantageous to them to minimize these costs or make sure that the price covered them. In order to simplify the problem of assigning the costs of breaking into schedules, a standard cost for breaking into schedules was determined and was used as a standard charge for accountability purposes. Account managers were now in the position of getting credit for higher margins, longer runs, and the elimination of "specials" (variations of products which are extremely costly in any plant), as well as for volume—again balanced accountability. They now developed an interest in production problems and for the first time willingly sat down with the cost manager to hear descriptions of the impacts of various sales procedures on the cost of production.

The impact of this change in recognition alone was enough to increase the profit from sales the equivalent of a 10 percent increase in sales—with no change in volume. As a sidelight on human nature, one account manager had a 90 percent decrease in "specials" from personal accounts with no loss in sales volume. At the same time this manager was adamant in arguing, "I'm not doing anything differently from the way I did it before."

Build Small Accounts to Make Future Large Accounts

One long-range profit problem that had existed in the sales department was that small accounts were not pushed. The problem is typical of any sales operation where most of the accounts are large. Account managers had been working on large accounts assigned to them and had not wanted to bother with small accounts; they had felt that the small accounts were not worth their time, especially when they were held accountable for volume. It had been natural for them to feel that small accounts were beneath them—that such accounts were not worth the time they required. Some small accounts could have become large in the future, however, and by that time competition would have been in solid. They, therefore, had to be developed currently. But the appraisals of the account managers had rewarded current sales, not future sales; developing accounts for the future had not seemed advantageous to the account managers.

In order to put more emphasis on small accounts, they were taken away from the account managers and given to assistant account managers as their personal accounts. The assistant account managers were then rewarded for the development of these small accounts. They put much more effort into developing these accounts because they had a personal stake in them.

Get Sales from a New Product Line

A special problem concerned a new product, a patented retail hardware item that the firm had developed. The product had not been related to the rest of the business; it had been a consumer item to be sold through retail stores instead of an original-equipment product. The same management approach had been applied to it, however: It had seemed natural to the executive committee to use the methods that had been successful in the rest of the business, even though the new product was a shelf item in retail stores. The sale of the new product had been placed under the vice president of sales, who looked upon it as a stepchild to the major line, expecting it to follow the same form of operation as the rest of the business. This approach had stifled the business; sales had been lagging. In addition, the manufacturing of the product had been placed under the manufacturing vice president. But the item was essentially plastic, and the main product line was metal. As a consequence, the manufacturing of the new product had not been done efficiently.

The management design for the new product was changed, and the item was set up as a separate division reporting directly to the president. The new division manager was given the authority to develop sales approaches to fit the retail trade and set up manufacturing to fit long, standard runs—overall, to establish a way of operating that fit the product. In other words, the division manager could do what had to be done to make the product profitable.

For example, the division manager could work with dealers in a way that was suitable to the kind of consumer business that it was. If manufacturing representatives were useful, they could be used, even though they were not used in the main product line. The division manager could job out manufacturing or product development as he saw fit. The president then made the division manager accountable for the overall profit and growth of the division.

It seems natural for companies that have grown up in one business to force the same successful procedures on a new business, even though they do not apply. A business myopia sets in. The result is almost always unsatisfactory achievement in the new business. This lack of executive flexibility is often the reason why successful companies cannot grow profitably.

DEVELOP PROFITABLE PRODUCTS

In order to maintain its position, the firm had had to constantly develop and adapt changes in its products to meet the needs of particular accounts. The requirements of one account might have changed differently from those of another account. This product variability is characteristic of an original-equipment-manufacturer (OEM) job shop, making it hard for an executive to exercise executive control and still be adaptive to the market.

Coordinate Product Design

Both the account managers and the engineers in the engineering department had done product design work. The result had been a great deal of duplication of design and, in addition, expensive nonuniform parts. Die costs had been high because of the limited use of many dies, coupled with the fact that many manufacturing runs had been short. The account managers had argued that they had to design to meet specialized customer requirements; after all, they had talked directly to the customers and had to meet any competitive proposal. The argument had seemed sound to the president. Any approach to uniform parts by the engineering department had, therefore, been difficult.

Design responsibility was changed so that the engineering department handled all the product engineering and the account managers controlled all the customer relationships. But the engineering department had the obligation to give the product service required by the customers. Engineering had to be made accountable for meeting customers' needs and for the cost of meeting these needs. Engineering was, therefore, encouraged to develop a whole system of uniform parts, leading to lower manufacturing costs; since it had design control, it could carry through accordingly.

The account managers in turn were given the responsibility for bringing in customer specifications, not designs—an important distinction; they were to find out what the customer needed from the part. Since they were now appraised by the profit from their accounts, they became interested in selling both standardized parts and normal schedules whenever possible. The setup made it advantageous for them to work closely with the programs of the engineering department.

Grow with New Product Lines

There was one final area that had been lagging, the area of new products outside of the normal product line. These had not been coming along very well because the president had felt it logical to combine research on new products with engineering for the normal product line in the research and engineering department. Since this was a job shop operation, there had been so many "hot" customer application problems on current products that it had been hard for the research and engineering department to get around to longer-range R&D on new products.

Because of its technical knowledge in the condenser business, the firm had had a special opportunity to do research work for the U.S. Air Force, where this expertise was needed. This situation would have provided an excellent way to develop further into the field with the expense underwritten by the U.S. Air Force. On the other hand, the firm could have made a major contribution to the U.S. Air Force because of its need for the company's high technical expertise in condensers.

In order to place more emphasis on the new products, the president decided to separate current product engineering from research. Application engineering was put under a chief engineer with the job of keeping up the product line for the normal commercial trade. Research was placed under a research vice president reporting directly to the president. It was given the mission of carrying a new product through long-range development into a profitable product. To build company know-how, the research department was encouraged to take government contracts. Interestingly enough, the logical person to head this research was the vice president of research and engineering—but the research group only had a third of the staff that he had formerly directed. He was naturally reluctant to have a reduced staff; the president had to sell him on the value of concentrating his expertise on this one area of the company. Four years later, 40 percent of the company's sales and 60 percent of the profit were on new items that came from this research department.

WHY WAS PROFIT TURNED AROUND?

Why did profits develop from the management analysis? First, the president changed the accountability system so that pressure on management people was directed toward greater profit contribution in each position. Rewards were then given for these profit contributions, not for alibis; management systems and bonuses were changed to reward balanced productivity. Committee systems gave way to individual responsibility.

In order to further encourage balanced results, the responsibilities of line managers were broadened to cover all the parts of the operation. The vice president of manufacturing then made plant maintenance, industrial engineering, scheduling, quality, and purchasing accountable for improvement in line effectiveness; through joint accountability they were encouraged to compromise specialized action for overall line results.

Since the sales department had a major impact on plant efficiency, the president placed account managers on a profit-on-accounts basis instead of on a sales-volume basis; they were, therefore, encouraged to consider manufacturing and engineering costs when selling. Growth in number of accounts was encouraged by assigning small accounts directly to assistant account managers. The lagging hardware line was given new impetus as a separate division reporting to the president; it no longer was required to follow inappropriate methods of the standard product line.

Balanced product design was instituted. High product-engineering costs of the old product line were brought down by giving the engineering department broader design control. It was made accountable for standardizing parts while still meeting customer needs. To design new products for the future, research was separated from engineering with the prime mission of developing new products; it was encouraged to secure outside research contracts to build in-house technical knowledge on advanced state of the art leading to new products.

There was no one simple way to encourage better profitability. Various losses had to be traced down to multiple causes and management actions in order to improve ROM. Many programs had to be changed to encourage smooth coordination between departments; compromise was the order of the day. What was the overall result? The aftertax return on investment went up to 25 percent in three years; at the same time the firm was growing rapidly.

3 Making Better Service Productive

In any kind of service operation, achievement comes primarily from making people more effective; a ROM approach is especially critical in making them more effective. This is certainly true in airline companies such as Inter-Global Airlines.

Inter-Global had domestic U.S. routes and, in addition, routes to Canada, the Caribbean, Mexico, and the Pacific. It was, therefore, an international airline as well as a large domestic airline. Competition was severe; therefore, it conducted a management analysis to improve ROM in its sales division in order to maintain its competitive position and improve it if possible.

DEVELOP MORE VOLUME THROUGH A PROFIT EMPHASIS

As in many sales operations, the principal emphasis at Inter-Global had been placed on current revenues or volume; in theory more volume was automatically supposed to mean more profit and a better position in the marketplace. It had seemed logical to the vice president of sales that a management system geared toward increasing revenue should be most profitable; after all, more revenue should have meant the filling of empty seats. The only balance that had seemed to be needed was a check on sales cost per dollar of sales revenue. The management system had been set up accordingly.

All Sales Are Not Worth the Same

While the reasoning had some logic, in this case emphasis on volume and sales cost per dollar of revenue had not necessarily geared the sales department to profit; at times it had actually been antagonistic to profit. For example, as in many airlines, volume had been highly seasonal. There had been a sales bulge in February that later declined; there had been another bulge in the summertime that declined in the fall; then there had been another bulge around Christmas that declined in January. Each seasonal bulge and decline had its own special characteristics and had to be analyzed separately.

In order to maintain cost control in sales, the sales department had been carefully checked by its cost per dollar of sales. This approach, too, had some logic. Running empty seats in the light periods had, of course, been very costly; much of the cost had been fixed cost. Every additional seat filled in those periods would have resulted in almost clear profit. As a consequence it would have paid to spend quite a bit more money to get an extra sale; the extra sale would have been worth more in profit in the light periods than it would have been in high-volume periods. For instance, certain ethnic groups might have been encouraged to make group trips in off periods, but the arrangements would have taken a great deal of extra work on the part of the sales department—therefore, higher sales costs per dollar of sales. The emphasis on sales cost per dollar of sales had been a definite deterrent to sales productivity in those periods.

Actually filling otherwise empty seats at any time would have been worth the extra cost. In effect, the emphasis on volume with cost per dollar of sales as a control had given an illusion of balanced accountability; it had not been qualitative in terms of profitable sales because it had actually militated against profit in the long run by discouraging the extra expenditures to fill empty seats in down periods.

The vice president of sales then changed the whole accountability program to give extra weight to profitable volume. In certain instances as much as triple credit was given for any sales made during down periods, and the computer was programmed accordingly; the profit potential was worth it. In this way the sales department could be given additional recognition for the tougher sales job and the increased profit to be obtained by filling empty seats in down periods.

Cancellations Are Expensive

Volume emphasis had another profit dimension. All the credit that had been given to the salespeople had been for sales made; no deductions had been made for cancellations. It had been assumed that sales districts could not control cancellations; they simply controlled original bookings. Besides, the sales department had been supposed to concentrate on selling, not on analysis to determine why people cancel. Cancellations had been very expensive, however; after the planes had been fully booked, cancellations had caused empty seats in what should have been full flights. As a consequence customers who had been refused reservations could have received service. In some cases cancellations had come from double bookings—customers booking on two flights for insurance of a seat. There had been little effort made by the sales department to discourage this practice.

The vice president of sales changed the evaluation procedure so that any cancellation was deducted from any sales credit given to salespeople or to district managers. Accounting records were changed accordingly. It was then advantageous for salespeople to do a more qualitative sales job—to make the sale stick. For example, they discovered ways to discourage double booking and so filled more empty seats.

PRODUCE REPEAT CUSTOMERS THROUGH TOP SERVICE

An important factor in maintaining and increasing revenue was customer satisfaction with service. If customers thought service was very good, they would be repeat customers, thereby increasing sales without adding to the costs; sales costs per dollar of sales would be reduced. The essence of any service business is satisfying customer's needs as they perceive them; it is the underlying requirement of a service business.

Encourage District Action

One deterrent to good service had been the slowness of the action on customer problems. Prompt customer action at the local level was sometimes hindered because a number of decisions were centralized; they had to be cleared with the home office.

In addition to slowing up decisions, the home office had affected customer service in another way; it had tended to focus on errors in a conscientious attempt "to help" the districts. The approach of home-office staff had consisted of carefully analyzing any deviation on reports and suggesting corrective action. They had not been familiar with the local problems behind the reports, however. Nevertheless, it had seemed logical to have home-office experts analyze problems because of the close interrelationships that exist in an airline. This thinking had naturally led to standardized computer reports to make comparative studies between districts. These standardized reports, in turn, had further discouraged people down the line from taking quick action, creating a negative impact on customers.

Using standardized reports to make home-office decisions is a common error in many operations; they seem so helpful for comparative studies. However, conditions are often slightly different from one location to another. Computer reports must take this into account, and judgment must weigh in local variations; standardized reports are frequently antagonistic to sound local action.

But the home-office influence had gone further. The home-office staff departments had been expected to approve a particular solution in their specialties; executives had felt that this approach forced a better "expert" analysis of a problem. But here fragmentation occurred; each specialist was not acquainted with the overall problem and focused only on a specialized part. The compromise of specialties needed to give good customer service had often been delayed. This process had put an additional stumbling block in the way of giving good service at the local level; the productivity of local people had been reduced.

In fairness we should point out that the nature of the airline business requires considerable central coordination to be most effective; after all, the districts have to work together as one airline. For example, careful scheduling of all flights is needed to get the maximum use of planes and to optimize service to customers. Reservations must be made on a systemwide basis, and all offices must be tied to a central computer. Passengers must be effectively transferred for connecting flights. Overall, an airline presents one image to the customer and a certain amount of centralization is necessary to strengthen the direction of everyone down the line toward good passenger service.

In order to achieve more sensitivity to local problems, the vice president of sales changed the emphasis of home-office people. Those who were involved in centralized customer decisions were made accountable for their impact on the local district operations where the customers were. The unique local problems were their problems.

Uniformity Does Not Increase Productivity

Districts also had difficulty in meeting their problems because of another aspect of uniformity: The vice president of sales had thought it only fair that all districts should be treated equally. The treatment had not necessarily reflected major variations in district problems or differences in size, however. For example, authority had been about the same for district managers of different-sized districts; "a district was a district" had been the philosophy. As a consequence, action in large districts had been strapped because the district managers had not had enough authority themselves to redelegate adequately to their subordinates.

Uniformity in delegation is a common problem in many firms; executives do not delegate more authority to managers of districts or plants of larger size. As a consequence the manager cannot redelegate adequately, and action is slowed up. At the same time, subordinate managers are not developed. The problem creeps in as the districts or plants of an organization grow; authority is not increased accordingly.

At Inter-Global, delegation was changed so that more authority was given to the districts. In addition, authority that was delegated to the large districts was greater than that given to the small districts. District managers could then make more decisions and delegate properly to allow people below to make decisions that would facilitate prompt customer service. Productivity increased because more time was spent giving service instead of consulting with home-office specialists. As we stated earlier, in order to tie in the home-office specialists better, they were made accountable in terms of local district results. They, too, were tied to customer effect.

Give Credit for Service Rendered

Another factor that had militated against giving good service had been the credit given to a district for transfer passengers— passengers transferring to another airline en route to their destination. Districts had only received credit in their budgets for passengers boarded; transfer districts might have done quite a bit of work to help get passengers through but got no credit for it. Transfers dragged them down. Some districts had many transfer passengers, while others had few. The budgets of transfer districts had been strapped, and their appraisals had been affected. As they had seen it, they could not afford to do a good job. The budget allocation was antagonistic to cooperation for service to a customer.

The vice president of sales had to get the budget director to change the allocation for transfers so that credit would be given to a district for any necessary service that was rendered to a customer. A district would then be encouraged to do the best possible job of moving passengers on their way whether they were originating passengers or transfers. Passengers judge an airline by the total service they receive.

What Is Reservations Productivity?

An interesting angle developed with the evaluation of reservation clerks. They had been given credit only for tickets sold for Inter-Global flights. The idea had seemed sound; it had encouraged them to place customers on Inter-Global flights as often as possible, even though this might have been inconvenient for some customers. After all, the function of sales was to sell Inter-Global seats. Of course, some customers had learned later about more convenient flights. They had then naturally questioned Inter-Global's concern about customers and decided to favor other airlines in the future.

The plan for giving credit to reservation clerks was revised so that they were given credit for any ticket written, whether it was on Inter-Global planes or those of any other airline. In other words, they were given credit for giving top service to the customer. Knowledge of this policy soon spread among the customers; they knew then that they could depend on Inter-Global to do the best for them.

There had been another stopper to good service by the reservation clerks. It had been difficult to evaluate the quality of their customer contacts because the contacts had varied considerably. The firm had therefore instituted an evaluation through a random monitoring check to see if the reservation clerks had asked customers certain critical questions, presumably the right questions. The evaluation technique had seemed logical since research had indicated that these questions were generally important in giving good service. The trouble with this approach was the word "generally." Each customer had called for a different reason and often had not wanted to, or had not needed to, go through all the standard rigmarole of questions.

The incongruity of this quality evaluation program was brought to a head when one reservation clerk was rated down because she did not ask some of the "critical" questions, even though she made a $700 sale and had a satisfied customer. What the system had really been doing was focusing on the theoretical need for uniform activity, not on the result—customer sales and satisfaction. It had been erroneously assumed that the rating reflected customer satisfaction. Like most ratings of that type, it did not; there had been too much variation in customer needs. Few customers were the typical "average" expected by the plan. Programs based on "standard" customers often fail; there are too many variations from the standard. The vice president of sales then changed the role of the reservation clerks and their evaluation. They were made accountable for quality of service as measured by customer feedback, not by questions asked in the interview. In addition, they were made accountable for their sales-cost ratio.

Get Customer Feedback

Since a service business is primarily dependent on customers' goodwill to get repeat business, it is always necessary to have strong feedback directly from customers. At Inter-Global there had been rather informal feedback from customers. Comment cards had been available at some locations, but they had not been freely available. They had not been a regular part of employee evaluation systems.

Comment cards were then made readily available in many more places so that any time customers wanted to say something good or bad about any part of the service, they could easily do so. In this way service was measured from the customers' point of view at the time when they were thinking about service. Customer comments were then worked into the evaluation of personnel. To assure frankness, customers were asked to turn these cards into a central department, not to the person giving the service; it is hard for a customer to say something negative about an employee to whom he or she is giving the card.

Upgrade for Higher Productivity

Service to a customer had depended on the accumulated work of all the reservation clerks, counter clerks, check-in clerks, and gate clerks. To be effective, all had to be trained and supervised in working together to satisfy a customer. But the company had not fully developed its first-level supervisors in supervising; in fact, under the organization philosophy that had existed, supervision had not been assumed to be their major job.

The supervisory capabilities of all supervisors were then broadened through training by the management development department. In addition, higher management designated direct supervision as the major duty of first-level supervisors. Beyond this, the latter were trained in how to train so that they could efficiently upgrade their people.

Supervision and training should be the prime responsibility of first-level supervisors in any operation. The first level is the base for the productivity of all higher managers, the place where their productivity shows up.

GET STAFF TO MAKE THE LINE
MORE PRODUCTIVE

A central marketing staff had developed and pushed uniform marketing plans for the system; this seemed the most efficient way to get a good marketing job done. After all, any customer might have used any part of the system. There had not seemed to be any sense, therefore, in having each district develop its own marketing plans—should each reinvent the wheel? It had been assumed, of course, that all district problems had been the same, or at least very similar; after all, they had all been selling the same seats to passengers. It is true that there had been some similarity between districts and, therefore, there had been some advantage in having uniform plans so that districts would not duplicate effort needlessly. However, individual customer requirements had varied between districts. Some deviation from master plans had been needed to fit these variations.

Develop Action Plans

Because of the centralized approach taken in marketing and the assumption that districts were similar, there had been little district input into central marketing plans as they had been developed. Districts and regions had merely reviewed the plans when they were completed. It had been assumed that this review gave the districts ample opportunity to influence the plans and any earlier review would have been unnecessarily costly.

It is a common misconception of executives to assume that it is enough for the line to merely review a staff plan after it has been completed—let the experts develop the plan. To the contrary, the line usually needs to be involved in the formulation of the plans in the first place in order to make a full contribution; staff people usually need the advice of the line on current local problems as the plans are developed to keep their thinking realistic on the many variations in these local problems. If plans are only presented to the line after they are completed, there is a natural reluctance on the part of staff to change them where necessary to fit local conditions.

On analysis a further difficulty in the marketing plans was discovered. The home-office staff people had usually presented a general marketing plan along with appropriate statistics to back up the plan, but they had not presented a detailed way to make the plan work. While there had been many informational meetings with district people on the marketing plans at which product knowledge had been disseminated, sufficient specific selling instruction had not been given. Many sales departments assume that dissemination of knowledge about products and sales programs is the same as developing and training salespeople in a way that actually gets more sales. It is not necessarily so.

The vice president of sales then decided to change the whole mode of operation so that the districts were involved in many of the original marketing planning sessions. In addition, he required that the central staff carry plans through to action plans. The action plans encouraged the productivity of local salespeople, taking into account the variation in local problems.

Let Staff Pass on Its Expertise

Since the home-office marketing staff had not been given the responsibility for action plans for the districts, it had not tried to upgrade the field people in their various specialties. It had felt that the training of field people had not been a function of staff but of the district managers. After all, the field people had reported to line supervision.

Many central staffs share this belief about staff's training responsibility. Executives have not recognized that the primary contribution of many staff functions to the success of the organization is through the spreading of their expertise so that it is applied effectively wherever possible. Staff should not simply be masterminds. Executives have not delegated a responsibility to staff to upgrade practical specialized know-how of line people.

Because of this lack of training by staff, the field people in the districts had not developed the expertise they should have. The problem had been especially noticeable in cargo freight. Most of the district management had advanced in the organization through passenger sales and had needed a great deal of background and skills training to be effective in cargo sales. It had been hard, therefore, for cargo sales management in the home office to get maximum effectiveness in the districts in cargo sales unless they upgraded the field people in cargo sales work.

The vice president of sales then changed the function of central staff people so that they were accountable for the results of applying their specialties in the districts. The broadening of district people in a staff specialty was made a prime function of the home-office staff. To encourage the home-office staff to carry through on this responsibility, the vice president of sales held them accountable for the effect of this training on line results. In effect, they were set up to develop the line to solve local line problems, not simply to give out procedures and plans.

CONTROL COSTS WITHIN THE OPERATION

Even with a realistic approach to sales, there still had to be cost control within the operation. Cost accountability had been spotty. While sales cost per dollar of sales had been closely monitored, districts had not been made accountable for the full cost of the district operation. A deeper analysis of costs was required.

Make Each Manager Carry His or Her Share

First of all, accounting had not charged the districts for all the facilities assigned to them, for the capital they had used, and for some of the services they had received. As a consequence district managers were not aggressive in cost controls. For example, one district had three sales offices in a particular town but only needed two. The district manager, who had not been charged for the extra space and cost, had not been held accountable for them. Since the pressure had been for volume, the district manager had figured that there might just as well be extra space—it would probably contribute to a few more sales even at a high space cost.

The vice president of sales then had the accounting made more realistic and made district managers accountable for all costs incurred for their districts. District charges included all costs of space, facilities, and services used. It was then advantageous for them to optimize the use of these.

Fluctuate Costs with Demand

A subtle problem had been generated because the vice president of sales had approved personnel complements and facilities based on peak demand. The approach had seemed logical because the sales department had wanted to assure top service to customers at all times. In normal or low periods they had, therefore, been overstaffed; in a sense, they almost always had excessive cost. Costs had been somewhat insensitive to fluctuations in demand.

The vice president of sales then changed this philosophy so that districts were made accountable for total cost compared to sales (with adjustments for light periods mentioned earlier). They then set up facilities and personnel complements based more on average demand but found ways to expand temporarily in peak periods.

Build on Satisfied Customers

Baggage complaints had developed an interesting problem. Central complaint procedure had required that a local sales representative would go out to the customer, see the damaged bag, fill out a complete form of information, and send it to the home-office claims department for determination. The claims people, in turn, had then decided on the amount of the settlement and subsequently had sent out the check.

First of all, the procedure had taken quite a bit of the sales representative's time. The form had been, of course, respectably long ("might as well get complete information as long as you're going"). In addition, quite a bit of time had elapsed before a decision had been made. In spite of the extensive information form, the claims department frequently had felt that they needed more information to make a sound decision. The sales representative then had to go out to the customer again, get the additional information, and send it in to the claims department. Strangely enough, the attempt to save money had resulted in a considerable extra cost in carrying through on the whole process. In the meantime the customer had become more and more dissatisfied by the whole operation, resulting in considerable ill will over something that should have been semiautomatic. The procedure resulted in an overemphasis on the immediate cost of settling the claim.

This preoccupation with the apparent cost of settling a claim while ignoring the overall effect is typical of many service companies. The total cost is often increased by the process.

The claims procedure was revised so that a sales representative was given the right to make any settlement under $70 and (very important) to make the decision on the spot; it did not have to be cleared with anyone. The new process took considerably less personnel time and was less cumbersome. The customer was much more satisfied with the whole process and felt Inter-Global was a fair company.

Contrary to the expectations of the claims department, the new procedure often resulted in lower settlements; claims people had feared that the sales representatives would give the airline away. However, when the representative said to a customer, "Your bag is obviously damaged. What do you consider a fair settlement?" the customer was likely to say, "Well, it was an old bag, I think it was only worth perhaps $40." When the salesperson said, "I'll send you a check tomorrow," the customer felt good about the company.

WHAT WAS NEEDED

In this analysis it became clear that the key to success was service to the customer. But service was made up of many bits and pieces. Every contact customers had with the company reflected the kind of service they were getting. The president had to analyze every part of the operation to make sure that it focused on customer needs. The accumulated total of many small items made up good service. Good service was the basis for ROM.

Where did the analysis of service lead?

It lead to the establishment of procedures that viewed all customer service as important, including interline transfers. It emphasized quality sales—few cancellations. Supervisors were trained in effectively supervising customer relationships. It became clear that only local people could give service, so local initiative had to be encouraged. The analysis pointed out the need for decentralizing authority to the districts. Even many complaints were then settled by the local sales representative.

The analysis went deeper and resulted in gearing reservation clerks to satisfying customer needs, instead of asking a standard list of questions; they were made accountable by customer feedback and tickets written instead of by a monitoring of customer conversations.

The analysis then tied in home-office marketing staff to help local district people service customers. It became clear that marketing plans had to be action plans with heavy line input to be relevant to customer problems. Central staff was also encouraged to pass on its expertise so district people would be more effective.

The analysis pointed out the need for balance in attaining profitability. Districts were made accountable for all their costs in giving good service, including those for facilities and for fluctuations in personnel. The emphasis on volume was changed; special emphasis was given to profitable volume when planes were empty. Good service then led to increased ROM.

CHAPTER 4

A Small Company Steps Ahead

Small family firms present some additional aspects in getting good ROM. Their objectives are usually different from those of large companies. Such firms are usually the result of one-person operations; in the process of growth they develop in a somewhat unsophisticated manner. They are often very proud of their informal management approach, stating that they "will never get like a big company" and lose the family feeling—the feeling of oneness with their employees. When they get larger, however, circumstances overcome them; they discover that they must institute some of the same kinds of practices they decried in the large companies. In general they are unprepared for these practices.

Small family companies have the additional problem of family succession. Ordinarily, they wish to develop somebody in the family to be the future head of the company. As often as not, that person has not been trained through working on a series of accountable jobs the way a professional manager would have been in a nonfamily firm.

A good example of the problems faced by family firms was the Jones Company. It was started by Howard Jones, who owned 100 percent of the company. Howard had never gone to high school, but he had acquired a considerable amount of shop savvy through working in various shops and, in addition, had excellent business acumen. The firm had grown slowly to 150 employees. It had no debt. At one time in the past, Howard had been into the banks deeply; when times got a little rough, he always remembered the searing experience and resolved never to get into debt again.

Because at the time there had been no one in the family to advance, Howard promoted his protégé, Raymond Kelly, to the presidency of the company. Raymond was grateful for everything that Howard had done for him. Howard's only son, Tom, was a graduate mechanical engineer. Although Tom had worked in the company for several years, Howard did not feel that he was ready to be made president and, in fact, wasn't sure that he would ever be ready. However, Raymond, out of a sense of loyalty to Howard, wanted to develop Tom to be president to replace himself some day.

A reexamination of the company's management process was triggered off by a union election. The plant had been nonunion, and like most heads of family firms in that position, Howard had prided himself on having no union; he had felt that it was a reflection on the management of a company to have a union. He had believed that a union would be expensive in the troubles it might cause, even excluding a strike possibility. To the surprise of the management of the Jones Company, although the company had won the election, it had won by only 54 to 46 percent. Experts in industrial relations advised management that when the next election was held, in another year, the union was likely to win.

Strangely enough, the plant had high morale. Later on, when a consulting industrial engineer was brought into the company, he found many places where employees were working at 110 percent efficiency on a day rate (no incentive pay). It is almost unheard of for employees to work above an 80 percent pace when on a straight day rate. In general, employees had been very loyal to Howard; poor morale had not caused the swing to the union. What had seemed to be affecting employees had been the fear that they would not get the same consideration when Howard was gone—they might be pushed around. In addition, the company had accumulated substantial profit sharing money in trust for employees. Many employees had felt they wanted to get their hands on that money right away, and this attitude became a factor in the union's eventual success.

Howard and Raymond were faced with a difficult decision. On the one hand they could have spent the next year trying to do everything legally possible to prevent the union from coming in; with the high morale they might have had a good chance of being successful. The alternative was to spend the next year reanalyzing all their management and personnel processes and correcting any problems with the thought that whether or not the union won, the company would still be in an excellent position to manage well for high ROM. They decided to take the latter course.

Since much of the expertise the company might need in carrying through on this project was not in-house, they decided to carry out the program using outside consultants. Small companies need the same high expertise in various specialized functions that large companies do; they just do not need as much of it. They do not need permanent experts. Used intelligently, consultants can give a great boost to a small company in changing its whole management process.

Howard and Raymond then decided to carry through on a total management analysis of the company, with the idea of putting the company into the best possible position for high ROM with or without a union. The second major objective of this analysis was to develop Tom to be an effective future president and to establish a good management setup that would be workable for him when he took over. In line with this approach, Tom, who had been working in various production capacities in the plant, was made vice president of manufacturing.

IMPROVE THE
PERSONNEL APPROACH

Since the management analysis was triggered off by the union election, the natural first point on which the analysis focused was the improvement in general personnel approaches. Raymond decided that they should review every approach to managing people in order to keep a smooth efficient operation. He wanted to maintain the high drive for productivity that they already had (as indicated by the 110 percent application), improve their methods, and reduce employee fears of being pushed around.

Develop Foremen as a Bulwark

Although the company had been profitable, it had never been extremely profitable. The most it had made was 10 percent profit after taxes on the investment. As a result of the analysis Raymond did not feel that this profit was satisfactory if the company was to be a solid one and grow. The first objective was to lower unit cost in production.

One of the reasons why costs had not been as low as they could have been was that all first-line supervision in the plant had been carried out by lead people. These were hourly people who supervised others but also worked on machines themselves. Management had felt that they provided inexpensive supervision. However, as lead people they had not assumed full responsibility for training, stimulating, and guiding their people. They didn't have the time. They had not ordinarily been accountable for the accomplishment of their people, even though they had been a conscientious group. If the union were to get in, they would be in the union and might be restricted further from assuming a full supervisory responsibility. It would then be even harder to hold them accountable for carrying through on management's requirements. Since they had been the first level of supervision, their experience and interest had to be relied on to get a sharp operation.

In addition, the lead people had often supervised more hourly people than they could handle while doing their regular jobs as operators. Further, the management responsibility of lead people had been more or less generally understood but had never been clearly defined.

In order to get stronger supervision that Tom could rely upon in the future, Raymond decided to make all supervisors salaried people—management people who would not have production work to do themselves. In the event that there would be a union, they would still be considered part of the management team. Most salaried foremen were promoted from the group of lead people.

In order to assure the foremen time for supervision, they were set up with a limited span of supervision. They had about the same number of people reporting to them as the lead people had before, but they now had no responsibility outside of supervision.

The job of the foremen was then defined as primarily that of running the crew effectively. They were expected to do whatever would be necessary to accomplish this. In order to determine what was necessary, careful objectives were set for foremen, specifying what each was expected to accomplish in the year. The foremen participated in the setting of these objectives. To fortify the objectives, Raymond instituted a pay system that rewarded foremen for the accomplishment of these objectives.

Foremen were given the authority to supervise their crews, something that had not been done with the lead people. As an example of this authority, foremen were allowed to order any supplies or pieces of equipment that they needed up to $150 per item. The effect was immediate; one foreman was about to buy a broom and discovered that it cost $25. He hit the ceiling and figured out ways to use fewer brooms. While this was a minor item, it was indicative of the change of attitude that developed once the foremen were given authority and were accountable for their unit cost of operation.

The fact that these lead people were now called foremen did not suddenly wave a wand over their heads and make them operate like foremen. A number of changes were required to build them up. First, they needed considerable training in different aspects of supervision, so Tom made sure that each of them got this training; he, too, was trained in the process. As part of this training they were taught how to use the authority that they had now been given.

Since the foremen were now expected to train their hourly people, each was also trained in how to train. Beyond this, they were also trained to follow up on any training of their people, the most critical factor in any kind of training program. Since all the foremen were familiar with the operations that they now supervised, they did not need to be trained in the work itself.

Make Personnel Policy Invigorating

One of the problems that concerned Tom was that of minimizing the interruptions caused by employee problems, whether or not the employees were unionized. He wanted to be sure that personnel problems were taken care of properly. On the other hand, he recognized that an excessive amount of time spent on these problems would affect productivity.

It had been difficult for lead people to supervise their people because they had few policies to follow. The firm had defined neither its personnel policies nor its management policies. The analysis clarified the need for these policies. In order to provide Tom with a better management framework, Raymond decided to develop the policies more fully. Both Raymond and Tom spent a great deal of time with the executive group developing various principles of personnel policy as a guide for operation. In addition, they developed a guide of management principles that would be applied in managing the business.

If this new management style of the company was to be effective in the plant, the foremen needed to understand it. Meetings were, therefore, held with them to discuss the implications of the policies in depth; the foremen became well acquainted with both the personnel and the management policies of the company. They knew the mode of operation that was expected of them; they had a track to run on and could feel more confident that they were handling problems uniformly. No foreman wanted to be accused of being unfair to his or her crew.

Tom ran the training sessions for plant supervision on management and personnel policy. In the process he learned a great deal about the policies and developed a better understanding of the problems of his people.

In order to be sure that policies were well understood, a re-review was carried out over a period of a year. One principle was reviewed at each session each week using an example that had occurred in the plant as a basis for discussion. As a result everyone got a much firmer understanding of the principles.

Many small companies err in this regard. First, they frequently do not develop a personnel and management policy, a set of principles by which they expect to operate. Second, even if they have developed the policies, they do not train their supervisors on the polices; they simply send out copies. Third, after they have exposed supervisors to the policies, they do not take the time to re-review each of the principles with supervisors in light of the operation. Supervisors need this re-review to develop a firmer grasp of the principles in operation.

One of the problems that showed up in the analysis was that foremen were reluctant to enforce the disciplinary rules of the company. There had been twenty-five rules, and each rule seemed to have good rationale. However, nobody likes to follow rules. In addition, foremen found that they were interpreting each rule differently; yet no foreman wanted to appear unfair to his or her crew. Tom then met with the foremen and evaluated each rule with one question: "What do we absolutely need in order to run the plant?" If a rule seemed desirable but not absolutely necessary, they eliminated it. They realized that since no one likes rules, they ought to have only those rules that were needed for operation. As a result of this critical review, only four rules stood up. These were posted on the bulletin board with a clear explanation given for each. All the foremen accepted them and therefore applied them. There was a uniform application of rules for everyone, and employees generally experienced a lift from the elimination of the extra rules. Production was improved; all the extra time that had been taken arguing about the other twenty-one rules was now eliminated.

Raymond was keenly aware of the fact that the company had been getting good work application from its employees. He wanted to keep this commitment to company welfare; he did not want any new programs or policies to dissipate this feeling.

The corporate-staff personnel function had been part of the controller's job, which had also included accounting, office management, and other duties. The controller, therefore, had little time to give to personnel matters, particularly with the new emphasis that was now needed.

The organization was changed to reflect the new personnel emphasis. The position of personnel director was set up to meet employee needs and upgrade supervision throughout the company. Although the position was a companywide function, the personnel director's prime focus was initially on plant problems. The person selected for the job had been a machine operator and a sales correspondent and, therefore, had some plant insight as well as sales insight. Raymond also engaged an outside employee relations consultant to train this person to be a personnel director. At the same time the consultant trained Tom in personnel thinking.

This approach was counter to the one taken by many small companies that go outside to employ a trained personnel person. However, the inside person is knowledgeable about the company, its operations, and its people. With this background, he or she can be given personnel knowledge and often do an excellent job in personnel work.

Tom and Raymond decided that they wanted a setup that would solve legitimate employee grievances quickly. The foremen were, therefore, given additional authority to handle grievances; the training programs on policy that were conducted for a year were very helpful to foremen in approaching their employee problems. The policies themselves helped, and the examples used in the re-review meetings clarified the policies. The foremen had more assurance that they were in tune with company thinking; if there was some doubt, the personnel director was relied on to interpret policy.

Raymond and Tom made the decision that employees should be treated as company employees, whether they belonged to the union or not. They were entitled to know what was going on, and they would be treated as part of the company staff.

Employee safety, seniority, and grievance committees were set up; minutes were kept of their meetings and distributed to employees. This same practice was continued when the union came in a year later; the minutes of all union-management bargaining meetings were written up and distributed the next morning to keep employees informed on vital negotiations. By that time employees felt that it was a common communications practice and that they were entitled to know.

At first the union challenged this distribution of minutes as being inaccurate. In one of the early union-management meetings it claimed that an item had been misstated in the minutes. The company immediately put out a correction in which it stated that an error had been pointed out and that it was glad to issue a retraction. This gave the minutes even more credibility and also gave the company an accepted way to inform employees of its negotiations with the union. Because of the personnel director's special training and relationship with employees, the second contract negotiations were carried out in just three meetings and still resulted in a reasonable contract.

Give Employees Opportunity

In order to maintain high morale, Raymond wanted to promote from within as much as possible. In line with this philosophy a program was instituted whereby the personnel director interviewed all employees to find out what their ambitions were and what jobs they wanted to work toward. If it could be done, the company wanted to try as much as possible to steer each person in that direction.

During the interviewing program it was discovered that the head of the employee committee had almost obtained a mechanical engineering degree in night school; Tom decided to make him a foreman, and within two years he became the plant manager.

Another employee showed ingenuity in working up improvements in machinery. He had a peculiar insight—whenever he looked at a machine he automatically thought of ways to improve its operation. First he was made a foreman; later he was trained by an outside consulting industrial engineer to be in charge of industrial engineering in the firm. He turned out to be a top-notch industrial engineer. Ingenuity is often hidden in unexpected places; it should be discovered, developed, and fully utilized.

Raymond pursued this approach of considering the interests of employees so they would not feel that they were tied down or pushed around by the company. He and Tom set up a program whereby any employee with five years of seniority could leave the company with a leave of absence for one year to try out any job anywhere else as long as it was not the same kind of job that the employee was already on.

Raymond feared that many employees would take advantage of this policy and that the firm would lose many good people. In practice, only two people took advantage of it. One was a skilled tool and die maker who was (from Raymond's point of view) a troublemaker on the employee committee. The man decided to be a draftsman and moved to California. However, it didn't turn out well and he came back. But now he no longer had the same influence with his coworkers, and he left again. He wound up as a successful real estate salesperson, and he later said it was the best thing that had ever happened to him.

The other employee who took advantage of the program was an assembler who was an excellent worker but always seemed to have a sour disposition; everything the company did was wrong. He went outside, got some training in TV game repair, and started his own business. Tom saw him a year later and was amazed at his change of personality. He greeted Tom with a smile and he, too, said it was the best thing that had happened to him.

Even though no other employees took advantage of this program, the effect was substantial. This clause was later put into the contract with the union; the employees would not let it go. Now the employees felt that they "could" leave if they wished, but they were staying because they wanted to.

This approach is at variance with that of many companies

which have long vesting in various kinds of pension plans and a heavy emphasis on seniority that ties the employee to the company. It makes the employees feel as if they are in chains and very often leads to much of the dissatisfaction among hourly employees.

ORGANIZE FOR PLANT PRODUCTIVITY

Although the foremen were now set up to handle their responsibility, the analysis had to go further and tie in other parts of the company in order to maximize plant productivity. Staff functions and line functions had to be redirected to fit the requirements for increased high-quality productivity.

Use Industrial Engineering for Efficiency

Even though the firm had had a high application of its employees to their work, efficiency still had not been as high as it should have been. The analysis indicated that there had not been a steady stream of methods improvements to increase efficiency but that there were good opportunities for methods improvement. Many of the methods had been high-cost methods; management had not seen the need to constantly improve them. They had money in the bank, no debts, and were comfortable. However, they felt that improvements needed in the future might be opposed by a union if they got one; they, therefore, decided to improve methods now.

A consulting industrial engineer, brought in to improve the methods, trained a company industrial engineer (the foreman mentioned earlier) in the basics of industrial engineering so that the firm would have in-house industrial engineering capability. The consulting industrial engineer also taught Tom the basics of industrial engineering so that he could better direct the methods work. In addition, the consulting industrial engineer trained each of the foremen in work simplification. The foremen were encouraged to apply this training both because they were now responsible for the cost of the work of their crews and because they were given more leeway to take action for cost reduction. They improved many methods that did not require analysis by a skilled industrial engineer.

A special methods problem was presented by the automatic screw machine department. It had been supervised by a foreman who was very skilled in the work. He actually knew more about methods in that department than most industrial engineers; he simply had not had the time to work on new methods. He was now given an assistant foreman who directly supervised two-thirds of the people. The foreman kept the remaining people but took on the responsibility for improving methods in the department.

Many companies feel that foremen cannot do methods work. On the contrary, if skilled foremen are given methods training and the time, there is frequently no reason why they cannot improve many methods.

Finally, the consulting industrial engineer put in incentive plans for all hourly employees in the plant and trained the in-house industrial engineer to install incentive plans and keep them current so that the company could have continuity in the plans. In one year all employees were earning bonuses of between 15 and 20 percent based on sound industrial engineering standards and improved methods.

Keep a Quality House

The company had always been proud of the quality of its products. It felt that it had been a leader in the field in quality; it wanted to retain that quality but to do so at lower cost.

Inspection had been generally done by the assembly department. The analysis indicated to Tom that he should change this procedure so that the foremen would be expected to do their own inspection and to be responsible for their own quality. Their objectives were set up accordingly. The chief inspector also made spot final inspections. In order to be sure that inspection methods were kept up to date, a quality control department was also set up. It was the job of the people in this department to develop and improve methods for checking quality, to help the plant people apply these methods, and to make spot final inspections. They did not supervise the inspection work itself, but they were made accountable for the quality of the product turned out as well as for waste. Thus they were made accountable in a balanced way for helping the line people be effective.

Control for Minimum Inventory

Raymond had been concerned about the amount of money invested in company inventory, feeling that it had been excessive. There had actually been little production control and little control of inventory of raw materials or of goods-in-process. In addition, purchasing had been carried out by a general office employee who had another responsibility. This employee had not emphasized competitive bidding by the suppliers but had developed favorites among suppliers because this had been an easier way to take care of the purchasing work. Excessively large quantities had frequently been purchased, thereby increasing inventories. At the same time, the employee had taken little responsibility for inventory.

Tom was encouraged to change the organization by combining production control and purchasing under one manager. It was the job of this manager to buy the right materials, to have them in the plant when needed, and to keep inventories at a minimum.

Inventories were then based on their absolute need for production. Inventory control was made easier because the consulting industrial engineer had tied several machines together into line production. Each machine then required less goods-in-process ahead of it. Beyond this, foremen helped to keep inventories down because they were now accountable for their costs, and their inventory was part of these costs. The new production control department controlled work directly from orders to make sure that all the inventory requirements were realistic.

As a result of all these changes, there was a substantial reduction in inventory with no increase in shutdown time caused by lack of inventory.

BROADEN ALL MANAGEMENT

Raymond felt that management changes were needed in all the departments of the company, not just in those of the plant, if the firm were to maximize ROM. He, therefore, extended the management analysis to cover the other functions of the business.

Develop a Hard-Hitting Sales Force

A key function of the company was its sales operation. Raymond felt that the firm was not getting the profit from the sales dollar that it should. Even though Raymond was the president of the company, he had also been acting as general sales manager. Since he had also been directing the heads of other major functions, he had had only a limited amount of time to spend on sales problems, however. He had been unable to carry through on all the executive problems involved in devising and encouraging a good sales program. To get around this difficulty, he had formed a committee of the four regional sales managers that periodically discussed sales problems and made decisions on the sales operation. Raymond had felt that he could keep on top of the sales operations in this way and still supervise the other functions. There had never been firm objectives for these regional sales managers; they had simply been expected to do the best they could to meet their problems.

Raymond then promoted one of the regional sales managers to general sales manager and appointed a new regional sales manager to replace the promoted one. The regional sales managers were responsible for setting estimates and objectives for their regions. Based on their proposals, individual objectives were then set by the general sales manager for all the regional sales managers. This action gave the sales function a stronger management direction.

In addition, sales policy and overall sales goals had never been defined or written down. The president had never had the time to do it. Now he worked out overall corporate sales policies and goals with his general sales manager and the regional sales managers. These policies and goals were distributed and explained to all of the salespeople. Now they, too, had a track to run on.

The accountability systems in sales, both for the salespeople and for the regional sales managers, had been based primarily on volume. This approach is common in many sales departments, particularly in small companies. In a small family firm like Jones Company, emphasis on volume alone presents added problems. Some of the products manufactured in the plant had a 20 percent profit margin, while others had a 10 percent margin. Some products had a 0 percent profit margin; in order to fill out its product line, the company had acted as a distributor on these products, which were manufactured by other companies. By the time the other companies' profit had been taken and all the expense required to stock and distribute these products had been charged in, there was a zero profit in them. These products had been kept in the line so that salespeople could hopefully sell the other, profitable products.

Raymond changed this system of credit for salespeople. Credit was still given by volume, but volume was divided into three categories based on profit. All items that had 20 percent profit were counted as double in volume, those that had 10 percent were counted dollar for dollar in volume, and those that had zero profit were not counted at all. Obviously, the salespeople objected to receiving no credit for these sales. They were told, "We only have these items available to help you sell the profitable items; if they don't help, don't sell them." They couldn't argue with the logic. Within a year there was an 85 percent drop in the zero-profit items; at the same time there was a 15 percent increase in the 10 and 20 percent items. Obviously, salespeople had previously been putting effort into selling the zero-profit items. As a result of this change in the product mix sold, the company was able to cut the finished goods inventory of nonmanufactured items substantially and with the acquiescence of the sales department.

Push New Products

Raymond now turned the analysis to new products. There had been no new products for quite a period of time. They were needed, however, for the continuity and for the growth of the business. Raymond was concerned about this deficiency. All technical work in the company had been carried out in one department, whether it was for product development or for plant production. This approach is common in most small firms because they do not have many technical people. Raymond decided to break up engineering by separating product engineering from plant engineering. The new product engineering group was made responsible for developing new products that would sell, giving new emphasis to new product development.

Keep Managers Informed

Management action on many problems had been slow. One of the main reasons for this lag had been that management people, although conscientious, had not been fully informed about problems early enough.

The management information system had followed the typical accounting approach; it had been set up in order to fit financial statements. Little current data went to managers at various levels. Plant supervisors in particular had received little relevant data on their operations. This approach was understandable because they had been primarily lead people and had not been fully accountable. In addition, it had been hard for the accountant to know what information to give to each manager since managers had not had firm objectives. Raymond decided that all management people should be placed on objectives.

With objectives set, the information system was changed to management accounting; the computer was programmed to give managers important data that they currently needed in order to make the decisions that were necessary to meet their objectives. In fact, managers now demanded this information.

Most foremen now had a cost-per-unit objective. Part of the cost they were charged for was the cost of space and equipment that their crews were utilizing. They were, therefore, encouraged to use space and equipment efficiently and to get rid of anything inefficient. One foreman alone got rid of one-third of his equipment. By charging the foremen for equipment used, they were, in a sense, put in business for themselves. They got information that was helpful to them in meeting their objectives, and they were encouraged to make their own decisions.

Equipment and space are expensive. In many companies it is common for the foremen to give little attention to the space and equipment responsibility. There is an assumption that they can do little about these items. Under these circumstances, it is natural for foremen to hang on to as much equipment as possible with the thought that someday they might need it. It merely depreciates and is finally worthless.

HOW A SMALL COMPANY IMPROVED

This analysis of a small family company had to develop a different focus from that of an analysis of a typical larger company. The union organizing drive had clarified the need to change from informal, paternalistic management to professional management. The change was shown to be necessary for maximum ROM, for the successful growth of the business, and for sound succession.

The analysis led naturally to the development of management and personnel policy as a basis for the change in management approach. It further pointed out the need to reeducate all the management people in this policy and in the methods to effect it. To make the program work, the position of personnel director was set up to ensure the approach was carried through even with a union. This personnel position was necessary to solve employee problems without alienating loyal employees. Part of the personnel director's job was to train foremen to solve problems on their own. All the management and personnel changes were instituted under the guidance of a management consultant.

Improved productivity required new methods along with plant incentive plans. Since the firm needed high industrial engineering expertise, a consulting industrial engineer was engaged to guide the work. The consultant also helped set up new controls on raw-material and goods-in-process inventories so that inventory investment could be reduced.

It became clear that informal quality control would not be adequate for future growth, so a quality control department was set up. To make sure of day-to-day quality, foremen were now made accountable for the quality of products going out of their departments.

Sales were vital. The analysis detected a weakness that had developed at the top of the sales operation as the company had grown. A general sales manager was added. Balanced objectives were set for all salespeople, based on profit realized on products. The sales department was then geared to push profitable sales and growth.

It became clear that new products would not be developed if all engineering were to remain combined as it had been when the firm was smaller. Product engineering was, therefore, separated from plant engineering with the mission of developing profitable new products.

Information was needed by all managers in order to make the transition from an informal family firm to a modernly managed one. The practice of keeping information confidential had to be eliminated. Management people were now informed on what was going on. The record system was changed to a form of management accounting so that all management people received the information they needed to make decisions appropriate to their jobs.

On most of the new programs the company used consultants in order to temporarily command high expertise. In the main, these consultants trained company people in the new techniques and upgraded the prospective president, Tom.

What was the effect of this program?

Tom and Raymond got their management people together and collectively decided that they would like to make a 20 percent annual net return on the investment within five years; they had not made more than 10 percent up until then. At the time they felt this goal was "pie in the sky." But under the new management program the goal was met within three years. Tom was later made president.

CHAPTER 5 Make Cooperation Enhance ROM

Amost all operations today are fairly complex, requiring considerable cooperation between people to get maximum ROM. Failures in cooperation often come as a surprise to many executives; they do not understand why employees do not see its increasing necessity. Executives then jump to the conclusion that people are no longer as cooperative as they used to be—they are different. However, people today are not very different from those working a few years ago; it is usually the management climate set up by executives that causes the problem. The management setup has not changed adequately to meet the changing requirements of cooperation.

ENCOURAGE, DON'T DICTATE, COOPERATION—MAKE IT ADVANTAGEOUS

A common executive mistake is to assume that cooperation can be ordained by executive order. Executive orders do not force cooperation; frequently, procedures put in to help cooperation actually exert pressure against it. Rigid controls do not encourage accomplishment; they apply pressure to prevent a deviation. But deviations (the other person's too) are normal when working with someone else. Cooperation consists of blending so-called deviations; a management analysis should point out where it is needed.

Some executives rely on job descriptions and functional statements to force cooperation by meticulously describing the relationships that are expected. But descriptions by themselves do not establish cooperation; by themselves, they rarely inspire compromise. Instead, a management design must be developed to make necessary cooperation advantageous to those people who should cooperate. Even so, cooperation alone is not enough; the cooperation must be directed toward expected results. In short, it must be worthwhile to the people cooperating to compromise their specialties for the accomplishment of a needed result. Why should you expect people to cooperate if such behavior does not seem to be in their best interest?

MINIMIZE COMPETITION BETWEEN EMPLOYEES FOR HIGHER ROM

It takes considerable coordination to get people to compromise their own areas for overall results. It is more comfortable for people to ignore other areas, particularly since executives have often encouraged competition between employees. The rationale is that people will fight to do a better job (a sort of internal free enterprise system); for example, in filling a higher position, management can select only one of the aspirants. To the contrary, ROM is usually increased by minimizing internal competition in favor of cooperation. Competition does not favor cooperation.

"One Result—One Person" Makes for Better Compromises

As a first step in solving a cooperation problem, why not eliminate competition by eliminating the requirement for compromise; combine the work in one person. The best way to organize work efficiently is to ask one person to get one result alone, if the person has reasonable competency and training. Everyone knows this except, perhaps, the specialists. Why is it true? One person doing an entire job does not need to tie in with anyone else to accomplish the job. The person may not be an expert in all parts of the work but can frequently gain more than enough knowledge to overcome this deficiency by being accountable for blending the various parts of the work—for making the appropriate compromises between specialties without coordinating meetings. To make this delegation work, however, people must be accountable for results, not for carrying out the various activities. Otherwise, they may still pursue only partial solutions.

A simple example of combining work at a basic level was a short-run stamping firm that favored a management philosophy of organizing work by specialty. They had setup people set up the presses for the operators; the operators then simply operated the presses. It was assumed that setup work required special skills and that it would pay to have highly-trained setup people. However, when their presses were down, operators wasted a great deal of time waiting for the setup people. In addition, if anything went wrong later in production, there was a tendency for the two groups to pass the buck back and forth. The operators claimed the setup was wrong, and the setup people pointed out operator deficiencies in running the presses.

The plant manager simply combined the setup and operating work; operators were trained to do their own setup work. Each operator then did all the work necessary to turn out good stampings. The firm got a 10 percent improvement in productivity from the presses, plus the saving realized from eliminating the setup people.

Often the main reason so-called job enlargement seems to work is simply that all the work required for a result has been combined in one person and that person can then be made accountable for the total result.

Paperwork often lends itself to the same solution. In a steel warehouse, twelve people handled an order before it was finally sent out. The work was combined so that only three people worked on each order; each person did four parts of the work. It required an unconventional, circular work-station design. Staff was cut 40 percent, and the time required to get an order through the office was considerably reduced. There was less paper handling. Incidentally, it was also easier for management to locate an order in process. One of the reasons a computer installation often shows savings in personnel doing detail work in large offices (such as a life insurance office) is that it forces combinations of work. The work had previously been broken down by misguided management assumptions that efficiency results from specialization to minor work elements. The losses in paper handling, extra scrutiny, and work-flow control had more than eaten up the apparent gains of specialization. Sometimes the improvement in efficiency resulting from the computer could have been realized by simply combining work.

Give a Manager a Broader Result for Better Coordination

The same philosophy can be carried a step further. In any plant, try to place functions that depend on each other under one superintendent. Then it is up to him or her to see to it that all functions work together. For example, in machining let one superintendent supervise all the work to be done on a casting; in addition, assign a methods engineer, a scheduler, and a cost clerk to the superintendent's crew.

To simplify coordination, dissimilar functions may be combined under one manager even though they require different skills. A superintendent who supervises all the work on a product may be made accountable for blending all of this work. Accountability will make it advantageous for the superintendent to get all the functions to cooperate.

The same approach could apply in sales where product managers may supervise their own sales force, market researchers, inventory managers, and engineers. They would then coordinate all toward maximum profit and growth. They would really be product sales and marketing managers.

Small operations try to copy big companies and inadvisedly set up many specialized positions. The practice unexpectedly often reduces ROM. This was true in a small plant where management set up both a personnel director to help supervision on personnel methods and an industrial engineer to maintain incentive plans. There was constant controversy on union problems between the industrial engineer and the personnel director.

The personnel director was then trained in incentive work and was given the incentive responsibility along with the personnel work. Besides eliminating one person, the industrial engineer, the combination cut out the controversy that had existed. One person now had the responsibility of achieving employee efficiency through good personnel and incentive methods.

Even in technical functions the same principle applies. While organization by discipline (chemistry, physics, electronics, etc.) is helpful in solving some difficult technical problems, it can be divisive in completing some projects. Whether the specialized emphasis is necessary or not for a particular project, each technical person becomes immersed in his or her specialty and pushes it to the limit irrespective of the other disciplines involved.

On some projects an experienced technical person may be able to do the work required in several disciplines and compromise between them. For example, an experienced mechanical engineer often knows enough about the electrical and structural engineering applied in a company to carry through on them on many projects. The reason why strong control by project managers works well is that they can decide compromises between disciplines and force cooperation. We should emphasize, however, that project managers should not be set up as general coordinators. They should have authority to control projects and should be accountable for project results; otherwise, cooperation between disciplines may still be poor.

The essence of the philosophy of divisional organization is that division managers are put in charge of total businesses; it is their job to synchronize all the parts of the division and be accountable for its overall business success. Divisional organization or the combining of dependent functions under one overall manager of a unit improves operation because cooperation problems are simplified. Such managers are encouraged to make the compromises necessary to blend the work of diverse specialties for maximum divisional ROM; they do not have to rely on the cooperation of many central staff people.

Make Promotion and Sales One Result

A cooperation problem occurred in the sales operation of a company where new products were promoted by special promotion people in the same territories as the regular salespeople. The implied rationale was that promotion work required special talents and extra time. There were always considerable opposition and jealousy between the two groups, however; the regular salespeople resented the intrusion of the promotion people and did not follow up on their work.

The program was changed so that the field salespeople were trained to do their own promotion work. More field salespeople were added to provide the extra time needed for it. They were then made accountable for total accomplishment in their territories. The return from the promotion work was greatly increased; for one thing, the critical follow-up on the promotion work was carefully done because the same person did it and got full credit for it. There was no longer competition between regular salespeople and promotion people.

Get More for the Advertising Dollar

The same problem occurs in staff functions. The advertising department of a large company was organized by specialty; each of the media (TV, radio, slick magazines, newspapers, and so forth) was assigned to a specialist in that medium. The logic was clear: Each individual advertising person would be more skilled concentrating on a specialized area of advertising and would, therefore, do a more professional job. But there was considerable fighting for advertising budgets among the specialists. Each wanted the budget irrespective of whether or not it would get the most sales from the advertising dollar for the particular product.

The organization plan was changed so that advertising directors were set up for each product line. They were responsible for all the advertising for the line in any medium and had the obligation to secure the best sales value from each advertising dollar, no matter where it was spent. They were then more willing to make appropriate budget compromises between newspapers, TV, and so on; they were accountable for total sales accomplishment from all advertising for the product line. Interestingly, they looked with more favor on cheap local advertising aimed at special pockets of potential customers. Previously, the cheap local media had been given little consideration; it did not have the thrill of big national advertising.

MAKE REWARDS ENCOURAGE
PRODUCTIVE COOPERATION

It is the characteristic of many executives to delegate by individual accountability—hold the person accountable only for what he or she did; it seems unfair to hold the person accountable for what someone else did. They then rely on coordination from the manager above to get the combined result from the several people who may be involved. Such a system is a weak way to get day-to-day compromises between people for greater ROM; it actually reduces initiative toward results. Why? With increased specialization more specialists become involved in a problem; as we indicated before, each pushes his or her specialty and expects recognition for the specialized activity. Cooperation between them then becomes more difficult, and antagonisms develop. Each specialist fights for his or her own area whether or not it is the most effective way to get overall results for the organization. Even colleges are affected by this tendency; individual college professors emphasize their specialties, often regardless of the effect of the specialized emphasis on the holistic education of the student.

When individual initiative is pushed too far, it is counterproductive. It has a distinct point of diminishing returns. Beyond that point it detracts from the accomplishment of others in any cooperative endeavor. To prevent the attendant losses from individual drive not directed toward overall results, managers must direct individual initiative into cooperative channels toward results; they must force compromise of the work of all concerned in a result in order to blend their efforts. The best way to get this compromise is to make cooperative results advantageous to each person involved; employees should be rewarded for results even though others contribute to them. Otherwise, employee competition can easily prevent accomplishment.

Question Unique Accountability

How do accountability systems that reward people only for what they personally accomplish create pressures antagonistic to cooperative results? One example is the way budget systems often apply unique accountability and, therefore, discourage cooperation. People on budgets do not want to put in a great deal of time on somebody else's work, because they do not get credit for it; at the same time they are using up part of their budget money. The reason for the problem is that budgets follow the accounting philosophy of charging an expense to only one account—unique accountability—even though two people must cooperate to get a result. In theory you cannot charge the same dollar to more than one account. The accounting books will not balance. Management by objective (MBO) systems have followed unique accountability; they tend to evaluate a person only by what that person did—the impact on others does not usually enter into the evaluation. Employee appraisal systems, too, emphasize unique accountability; they highlight what the person personally accomplished.

While unique accountability seems a logical way to get more accomplished, it actually tends to discourage cooperation, frequently the key to accomplishment. Cooperation means sacrificing part of one person's area in order to blend with that of another in maximizing accomplishment. In this age of specialization it is particularly important to make sure that the whole reward system rewards for cooperative results in order to harmoniously blend in the work of the various specialties.

Reward for Joint Results

How can the reward system emphasize cooperative results so that management productivity is viewed as joint productivity of several people? The reward system should be revised to make cooperation advantageous to the managers involved. People will do what is advantageous to them as they see it. A most effective way is through *joint accountability.* It simply means this: If two or more people have to cooperate to maximize a result, each should get the credit for the accomplishment of the result or the discredit for the failure to accomplish it.

Contrary to normal practice, you do not try to appraise what part each person played; that is unique accountability and leads to divisiveness. Instead, each gets credit for the total accomplishment; in this way the reward system leads to cooperation. It is a management design to encourage cooperation; it makes it advantageous for people to make the compromises necessary to get results, and compromise is the essence of cooperation and of higher ROM.

Make Committees Productive

The cooperation problem has special significance in committees and task forces that have become popular. These are frequently organized by default because cooperation was difficult to obtain by normal management coordination based on unique accountability. However, the accomplishment of these committees often does not come up to expectations because they lack that lubricant for cooperation, individual commitment to the overall result. Individuals on the committee do not gain or suffer because of committee accomplishment or the lack of it. Their appraisals and rewards are based on their normal work; they are accountable only for accomplishment on their regular jobs, not for the accomplishment of the committee.

For example, a junior board may be established in a company to plan a new product line. It seems like a good way to develop bright middle-management people and at the same time tap fresh ideas for new product lines. Members of the junior board are not credited or discredited later on, however, by whether the product line succeeds or fails; after all, the success of the product line is not viewed as part of their regular jobs, and in addition, they do not make the decisions on the product line. If this junior board experience is to be helpful to the company and also to develop the junior board members, appraisals should later include these joint results. The junior boards will then be more productive because the members will be more committed to its accomplishment. Their view of their role on the junior board changes.

I remember one company where a person came to the presidency with a strong feeling that committees were the way to force cooperation; that was the way he used to run his plants when he was in manufacturing. After he was made president of the company, he tried to apply this philosophy to the whole company; all decisions were to be made by a series of committees. Managers were relieved of accountability through the various committees which he had set up, and incisive action was dulled. As a consequence the company was falling apart; aggressive adjustment to market changes was reduced. Participation was the required mode of operating, without first assuring that participants were committed to the expected accomplishments of the committees. Whenever a problem occurred, it was discussed and a solution agreed upon by a committee. Since "all had agreed," no one was accountable. Committees can easily be a refuge for those employees ducking accountability. This president had to abolish most of the committees and reestablish personal accountability, whether employees worked alone or in cooperation with others.

MAKE STAFF WORK HELP THE LINE PRODUCE

Joint accountability has special application to staff people because their fundamental job is that of helping the line get more results; for the staff to be effective in doing this, cooperation with and by the line is vital. To get staff people to cooperate with the line, an executive must make it advantageous for them to do so. Executives should, therefore, give them credit, with the line, for line results; that is why they are there—to help the line get more results. They should be encouraged to blend their work with the line's work in order to increase line effectiveness. The old theory that staff people should be self-effacing individuals who never seek recognition leads to lower staff ROM.

Capitalize on Plant Staff

How does joint accountability apply to staff people? Take a plant maintenance department as an example. It is a staff department whose prime purpose is to increase machine running time. Why not, therefore, give the maintenance people credit for reducing machine downtime due to repairs, as well as for the cost of maintenance. "But," you ask, "isn't the reduction of machine downtime really a line responsibility?" Yes, the line should be accountable for downtime. But it is also the job of maintenance to help the line with this responsibility. It should, therefore, be made advantageous for each to cooperate with the other to minimize downtime due to repairs; both should be given credit for low downtime.

The same approach applies to other staff functions, for example, machine engineering and traffic. Each may have an impact on downtime but in a different way—engineering because of faulty design which may lead to high shutdown time due to frequent maintenance work and traffic because of downtime due to materials that may be delivered late or damaged. An executive should set up the recognition system for each group so that it is advantageous for each to cooperate with the plant line people as much as possible to minimize the downtime that each affects. If the traffic department does not deliver materials to the plant on time or delivers damaged materials, the output of the production department suffers. The traffic department should also be made accountable, along with the line people, for this loss. If the engineering department designs equipment which requires little maintenance, the department should be given recognition for it.

A plant controller was made much more effective by joint accountability. He had previously felt that it was his prime job to develop data on plant problems for the plant manager. Such a gestapo-type assignment is unfortunately typical of many controllers. Obviously, people do not usually like someone who is always pointing out their deficiencies to higher managers.

Fifty percent of the controller's objectives were then based on the combined achievement of the first-level foremen toward their objectives. Does that seem like a poor objective for a plant controller? Perhaps, but what happened? He then went down to find out what the foremen's problems were; he changed the programming on his reports to give foremen the information they needed. As a side benefit, he discovered that he could cut out one-third of the information that he had been producing before; it was not needed by the foremen. As a commentary, he was now actually serving the plant manager much better than before because he was now helping supervisors get results for the plant manager instead of simply reporting deficiencies to the plant manager as he had done before. His whole data base was more productive because he was using it effectively to help line supervisors be more productive; he was using his expertise more productively—to help the line be more productive. He became an accepted member of the plant supervisory team.

Industrial Relations Can Be Cost-Effective

An industrial relations director of a multidivisional company felt that it was his job to prevent strikes. In the process of union negotiations, therefore, he accepted very expensive contract clauses in order to settle contracts without strikes. He rationalized that they were the price to be paid for preventing strikes. The president then made him accountable, along with production people, for total labor cost per unit of output: the cost of wages, benefits, contract clauses, and strikes. He became a more effective negotiator in terms of the total results of the plant. He carefully considered the cost of fringes, work rules, seniority systems, wages, and other benefits on the cost of plant operation; he made sure that the total package was economically sound.

Sales Needs Good Staff Work

In a printing company one salesperson had been doing a poor job for a number of years. She was a creative type of individual, however, who was very skilled in working out overall proposals for satisfying all of a customer's printing needs. But in order to do this she needed time, help from the art department, and, in addition, comparative cost estimates on different ways to run jobs. The first difficulty was that the market research department had made a study which indicated that, on the average, unless salespeople made five calls a day they could not be successful. Obviously then, the sales manager set up five calls per day as a requirement for each salesperson. But this particular salesperson could not possibly make that many calls and do the creative job that she was capable of doing. She needed more time to develop a total printing plan for a customer. The vice president of sales then eliminated the call requirement so that salespeople could spend the time required to work up a complete proposal on an important account.

However, basic data for cost estimates on alternative ways to run a job had to come from the plant manager. In the past the plant manager had been held accountable for costs compared to estimates, however; this had seemed logical. Do you suppose he would have given a salesperson a rock-bottom estimate under these conditions? No, he had wanted a cushion in case he underestimated. In order to secure the plant manager's full cooperation, the president made him accountable for sales obtained on those accounts where he gave estimates as well as for his cost per unit —a plant manager accountable for sales. It was then advantageous for him to give salespeople competitive estimates.

A third requirement needed to be met: The art department had to help. But it had felt accountable for turning out good artwork for customers, *not* for developing art designs that sold jobs. It had to be made accountable for sales obtained *through* artwork and not, as formerly, simply for the artwork needed for orders. After these changes were implemented, the salesperson's total sales went up 50 percent. At the same time his profit margin went up from 6 to 8 percent; he was creatively developing better printing layouts for his customers. The total setup increased ROM.

In many companies product managers do not blend their work well with salespeople or with manufacturing people; the product managers fail to see that this tie-in is necessary for product success. Their cooperation with both groups can be improved if they are made accountable for total profit on their product lines. They are then encouraged to be in tune with manufacturing to keep costs to a minimum and also to tie in to the sales department to more effectively sell the product and achieve maximum profitable volume. They are then more interested in understanding local sales problems and developing techniques to meet them.

Credit Can Help Sales

In a large bank chain the accounts receivable officer made himself a hero by having a very low loss ratio. He failed to see that the higher rate charged was meant to pay for taking risks with accounts having questionable credit. Of course, when new companies he had turned down were finally successful and eligible for conventional loans, they would not do any business with this bank. The firms turned to the banks that had helped them when they needed it.

To get this accounts receivable officer in tune with the branch managers, he was first made accountable for an "optimum" loss ratio (you should expect a high loss ratio on accounts receivable loans). In order to maintain balance, he was also recognized for the number of firms on accounts receivable loans that later turned out to be regular loan customers. He then had the same goal as the branch managers—to build profitable volume in the present, and in the future.

Credit managers of many firms have a similar effect on sales. They overemphasize credit losses to the detriment of sales volume; their loss ratios loom up as all-important. Instead, they should compromise some credit losses for sales increases; the purpose of credit is to help get sales, not to prevent sales. One way to encourage credit managers to do this is to give them credit for sales increases; in other words, executives should make it advantageous for them to help the sales department increase sales.

The credit manager of a multibusiness company had applied the same credit standards to all of the businesses. One business sold products to high tech companies. Many of these customers were not financially strong but could grow substantially in a few years. The profit margins were high enough, however, to sustain some extra credit losses. The standard credit policy almost destroyed this business. The credit manager then set up different standards and controls for this business. They helped the salespeople make inroads into this potential by accepting greater credit losses, losses that were easily absorbed by the higher profit margins.

Staff Productivity Is Reflected in Line Productivity

In trying to get cooperation between staff and line, executives often forget that staff must be working on projects which fit the results expected of the line if the organization is to fully capitalize on staff skills and make the line more productive. In an airline, an expert market researcher developed a fine program for trips to California and even had district managers review the program and approve it. However, at the time the program was put into effect, the general sales manager was encouraging all sales personnel to emphasize European trips. The program failed because district managers did not push it. It takes line cooperation to make staff programs work. It is a waste of good staff expertise to have staff work on projects that will not fit the emphasis of the line.

In one large company, the facilities planning department was accountable for constructing buildings but not for making the equipment in the buildings effective. It was not, therefore, completely in tune with the plant managers who wanted the combination in order to turn out low-cost, quality products; the line people wanted the equipment and the building to blend in order to get the lowest cost output possible. The vice president of manufacturing had to make the facilities planning department accountable for the impact on unit cost of both the equipment and the building together so that the department would compromise where necessary to get efficient production.

To make sure that skilled staff helps the line achieve higher productivity, line objectives should usually be thought through first, before setting staff objectives; this applies to both short-range and long-range objectives. Only then can effective staff objectives be set to help the line be more productive; the staff objectives should be set to augment the achievement of line objectives. Frequently, executives set staff objectives independently of line objectives. Staff and line people can then easily be at cross-purposes, and the firm does not realize a full return from the work of the staff.

Get Line to Help Another
Line Be Productive

An area that is often given inadequate attention by executives, however, is that of cooperation between various line functions. Because line results can frequently be measured, they are assumed to be independent. This is not true, and an executive mandate for cooperation or participation does not necessarily get them to work together if their objectives push them in different directions. If one line group is to cooperate with another line group, it must be advantageous to do so. In many cases there is more at stake in line-line cooperation than in staff-line cooperation, but no special effort is made to make the cooperation advantageous to those who should cooperate. In modern complex organizations many line operations are heavily dependent on other line functions if they are to maximize productivity.

Line-to-line cooperation is especially important in plants. In a chemical plant a simple preliminary process operated on an overhead of $50 per hour. It had considerable effect, however, on subsequent work in a large processing unit with an overhead of $500 per hour. The preliminary department supervision was on a bonus plan based on the cost per unit of output in the preliminary department. Logical? Do you think the preliminary department would incur any additional cost even though it might substantially aid the large unit? No. The preliminary department had to be made accountable for dollars lost in the large processing unit where the work of the preliminary department applied. At the same time the budget of the large processing unit had to remain unchanged; in effect, *both* departments would bear the cost. If only one were charged, each would try to dump any special cost on the other. The situation would be antagonistic to cooperation. With both charged for the extra cost in the large unit, however, it was advantageous for them to cooperate for the best overall result. The same problem occurs in many metal working operations between machining and assembly.

In most plants purchasing has a similar effect on both downtime and plant productivity because of the availability or the quality of materials. A double accounting system should be devised here too. Operating people should be charged for the total cost of running, including all cost of downtime. In addition, the purchasing department should be charged for losses in production due to materials that were not there on time or were off quality; it should be given credit for reducing these losses. You do not usually know how much the operating people could have done to prevent the problem. Under the new setup, however, it is advantageous for both groups to cooperate to reduce losses due to materials problems. Operating people will try to keep purchasing better informed about materials needs; purchasing will try to conform to the requirements of operating schedules.

An interesting problem of cooperation occurs in the sales departments of over-the-road trucking and railroad companies because a sale may be consummated through either the buyer or the vendor. Salespeople are normally given credit for freight originating with the vendors in their areas. The salesperson in the territory of the receiver of the freight is therefore not encouraged to cooperate with the salesperson in the vendor's territory. Yet the receiver will often determine the carrier. Close cooperation between the two salespeople is often necessary in order to maximize sales. Salespeople will cooperate better if each salesperson gets credit for all business that either originated in the territory or was destined for it. It is then advantageous for the salespeople in the territories concerned to cooperate in getting business.

The decision on the suppliers of mechanical systems for a new office building might be made by the owner of the building, the architect, the engineering firm, or the mechanical contractor. In order to coordinate the impact on all four, a vice president of sales of a company selling air-conditioning systems for new buildings found it was advantageous to divide the sales credit into four parts. Part of the credit on an order went to the salesperson calling in the territory of the owner, another part to the one calling in the territory of the architect, another part to the one calling in the territory of the engineer, and the final part to the one calling in the territory of the contractor. Each could have a considerable effect on the sale. They kept each other informed and pooled their efforts to get an order; the setup encouraged cooperation and increased overall ROM.

An important area of line-line cooperation that is often missed is the effect of sales on plant productivity. Job shop operations like printing or original-equipment manufacturers are prime examples where this oversight occurs. The timing, type of order, and size of order have a considerable effect on plant productivity. The company can improve plant productivity if it appraises the salespeople on a profit-on-their-accounts basis and charges their accounts with all costs to produce their orders, including all the costs of specials and special timing. Do not take any of these costs out of production, however, or you will simply create a series of arguments on blame between salespeople and production people. It is surprising how much more sensitive salespeople become to the needs of the plant when they are appraised by the profit realized on their accounts. The approach increases the value received from sales expertise. I should point out that an executive must change the MBO system, the information system, and the pay system to reflect this approach to make it effective.

In many companies a sales department can have a substantial effect on idle machine time by the way it sells the product mix; small companies can be especially affected. One small company had three major production lines in its plant; if the company did not have balanced sales volume day by day to fit each of these lines, it would not be profitable, no matter how great the total volume. In this case the salespeople were made accountable for machine downtime due to lack of orders; the effect was to encourage them to get balanced sales as needed in the plant each day. To make the plan effective, they had to be given daily reports of order backlog by production line to help them get balanced sales.

Interdivisional Cooperation Leads to Higher ROM

Cooperation can be critical among business divisions of a company, particularly if there is an international division and several U.S. divisions. Ordinarily, the international division depends heavily on the U.S. divisions for product development, for engineering help, and sometimes for product knowledge for sales help; it seems logical for the international division to capitalize on in-house company know-how. It is assumed that the U.S. divisions would naturally want to help the international division. But why should they if all their measurements are based on U.S. volume and they get no credit for international sales? In addition, helping international would cut into their budget performance. They would have to spend their time helping the international division and would get less accomplished in their own divisions. It helps to secure cooperation if the chief executive gives the U.S. divisions some credit for sales of the international division, in addition to letting the international have full credit. It is then advantageous for the U.S. divisions to give highly skilled help to the international division and to help make the international division successful. The company ROM increases.

USE COOPERATION TO GET HIGHER PRODUCTIVITY

In analyzing any management problem, it is important to keep in mind that all enterprise is essentially cooperative enterprise. Different kinds of work must be blended to get maximum ROM; a management analysis should aim at getting the optimum blend. Four steps are helpful in solving cooperation problems:

1. Combine the work in one person if possible, thereby eliminating the need for cooperation; only one person is then involved in a decision. Even dissimilar work may often be profitably combined into one job.

2. Combine dependent functions under one manager if the first step is not feasible. A manager can then better assure cooperation between functions. On a broad company basis this step suggests divisional organization. Managers accountable for results encourage cooperation among their subordinates.

3. Make cooperation advantageous to all involved. We all do what we feel is advantageous to ourselves. To effect cooperation,

a management analysis should review all the forms of recognition and change them to make needed cooperation personally advantageous to those who should cooperate.

4. Use joint accountability where more than one person gets the credit or discredit for an accomplishment. The overall accomplishment of a group is then looked at as part of the work of each member. The analysis should review whether staff is working on results to which line is committed if staff expertise is to be used wisely. Joint accountability can also be used to secure cooperation between line functions. For example, sales can often be helpful in improving productivity in a plant. Committees and task forces can be made more productive if each member is evaluated by the group's results.

6 Developing Profitable New-Product Projects

Managing a new-product development project is essentially a problem in controlled innovation. At first blush this seems impossible in that you do not know what kind of innovation will develop or where. Can anyone tell where the Muse will touch? No, but since the work is done by people, it can still be managed for better effectiveness; even though product development is a risk venture, you can increase the ROM of each project. As a consequence, the costs of product development are reduced; the development work is more productive.

As an example, let us take a product-engineering department in a large agricultural equipment company. This department, one of several scattered throughout the country, had been designing large vehicles for agriculture. Several engineering departments at different locations might have been involved in any single product project. The president decided to conduct an analysis with the objectives of reducing the elapsed time on product development projects, of decreasing the applied engineering time, and of increasing the profit on products once they were launched in the marketplace. These are objectives which could well apply to almost any new-product department; progress measured against them will indicate the ROM of product development projects.

FOCUS ON PROJECT RESULTS

A critical problem in making project work productive was the need to get all engineers to focus on the end result of the project —profit on sales of the product when it was marketed. Technical excellency of the project work had not been enough to assure this result; the direction taken might have been wrong or the time required may have been too great.

Develop Customer Specifications

The first requirement of a project was to make the designs practical in terms of customer needs. Many engineers had been inclined to design the perfect vehicle technically, even though it did not solve customer problems (it may have satisfied the engineers' perfectionist engineering inclinations, however). The vehicle they designed might not have sold well because it had not met customer requirements. To better direct engineers, the chief engineer set up a system to make engineers and engineering supervisors accountable for the fact that designs met customer needs.

To make sure that a project focused on customer requirements, market specifications were initially needed that detailed what the customers would require of a product in service and accomplishment. What did the customers want the vehicle to do? Instead of customer specifications, product specifications had frequently been given by the sales department. These stated what salespeople thought the product should be, almost dictating design decisions. What was required instead were application specifications—what the product had to do in the field, as well as expected future-service requirements. These two sets of specifications are quite different. In addition, an expected sales price was required that would appeal to customers; this price, in turn, would indicate the targeted cost that had to be met. Sales was, therefore, made accountable for developing accurate application specifications so that new-product projects would have sound direction. As a sidelight, this predictive work to develop application specifications usually requires somewhat different skills from those needed for straight sales work, although both require customer "feel."

Design for Low-Cost Production

Meeting customer requirements was not enough, however. Before a profit could be realized, a product had to be developed that could be produced at a reasonable cost. The price was fixed by the marketplace irrespective of cost. One of the key factors affecting cost had been the expense of getting a new product into production after the design had been released to the plants; at times, break-in costs in plants had been catastrophic. Redesign had often been necessary for ease in manufacturing; in addition, new manufacturing equipment had often been required. Because designs were often late, excessive overtime had frequently been necessary to meet initial production dates. Design engineers had naturally felt that these problems were manufacturing's problems even though design may have caused them in the first place.

A critical requirement of a design was production practicality so that the product could be produced at a reasonable cost. The easiest way to produce a new product had usually been through the use of present facilities, if at all possible. Of course, it would have been easier for engineers to design a new product if millions of dollars had been available to invest in new plants and new machinery; the final cost of the product would then have been greatly increased, however. It takes engineering imagination to design various components so that they can be produced economically in the present facilities without major adjustments. In order to encourage this imagination, the chief engineer had to broaden the accountability of design engineers to include total profit on new products; they were then geared to low-cost production.

One of the difficulties in getting lower-cost products was that the executives had built a reputation for the firm as a quality house. High quality had been justified because it assured a good market share in a discriminating market. Quality is an excellent aim, but in any firm it must be balanced by cost. In this firm engineers could have gotten into a great deal of trouble if any customer service problems had occurred on their products; however, they had received little credit for cutting engineering or production costs. The pressures on the engineers had been primarily on quality so that was what they had emphasized above everything else. If profit was to be the end result, however, they needed good quality but could not overdo it to the point where high costs made products difficult to sell profitably. This problem is common in many technical companies; high quality is important, but it usually is costly. It must, therefore, be balanced against cost.

The critical question to be addressed by the company was, What level of quality did the customers need to achieve their results? Would additional quality give them added value? Quality beyond a certain point would merely lead to excessive cost with little additional contribution. Customer complaints and comments would indicate the level of quality needed. Engineers had to be made accountable for both the needed quality (complaints and service problems) and for a design that resulted in a product at reasonable cost. The chief engineer, therefore, had to set up an accountability system for engineers, balancing quality and costs to assure the most ROM from engineering time.

One of the problems that arose in making engineers cost-conscious was that full cost data on design work was not currently available to engineers as they went along on a project. They did not know where they stood against expected cost. Since quality had been primarily stressed, this cost data had not seemed important and no one had pressed for it. If design engineers were to take action that would increase the profit on new products, they needed this data; they needed it to control their costs. The chief engineer, therefore, got the controller to place a full-time cost accountant in the engineering department. In addition, the computer was reprogrammed so that engineers could get product cost information as they progressed on a project. Beyond this, the cost information itself had to be changed to make it engineering oriented—attuned to engineering problems —which is generally quite a feat in any accounting department.

Encourage the Focus on Profit

The fact that projects were set up on a profit basis did not necessarily mean that engineers would operate that way. They would naturally follow the direction of the formal and informal reward systems; people do what they feel is advantageous to them. The chief engineer, therefore, changed all the recognition systems (appraisal, pay, etc.) to encourage this profit focus; engineers were then made realistically accountable for accomplishment and dates on projects, as well as for the quality of the product designed. Accomplishment was interpreted in terms of a product or component that met customer needs and that returned a good profit when it was out in the marketplace. The latter meant that the product would sell well and that it could be produced at a reasonable cost in the company's plants.

Many companies talk about their emphasis on profitable products in their product development, but in practice their recognition systems do not reward accordingly. They do not reward product designers for the total effect of the product on the company; they tend to reward for a difficult-to-measure technical excellence instead. The profit emphasis is, therefore, weakened.

TIMING IS CRITICAL—MOVE THE PROJECT ALONG

Although product development had been essentially a long-term proposition (several years for each project), timing had still been a critical factor. For example, if a new product had been released in September, it would have been perfect for merchandising the following year. If the same product had been released in February, six to eight months would have been lost in the marketplace and sales would not have been made because the season would have been missed. In addition, competition would have been tipped off and probably would have come out with a comparable product by the next season; thus the value of the innovative items in the new product would have been reduced. Beyond this, the cost involved in the project would have accumulated interest for quite a while longer before payoff. Overall it would have been much harder to make the product profitable; poor timing could make it a loser. The analysis had to go deeper, therefore, into timing.

One problem with timing on projects had been the failure to recognize that in the term of a project a day is a day is a day (to paraphrase Gertrude Stein). Understandably, it had seemed hard to become concerned about a day or week lost in the first part of a three- to five-year project. The final release date had seemed so far away; there had seemed to be ample time to complete the project. It had appeared to be a little ridiculous to push a project along so early; no special effort, overtime, or other expense had seemed justified to do it. There had, therefore, been little timing pressure on engineers in the first half of a project. Under these conditions a project had often moved more slowly than planned and, as a consequence, engineers had lost extra time waiting.

However, any time lost at an early date in a project could have had the same negative effect on final release dates and, therefore, start-up costs, as time lost later on. Like time lost at the end of a project, time lost early in a project could also have caused extra delays at the end of a project. The delays, in turn, could have caused a great deal of overtime, excessive cost (engineering and production), and sometimes even sloppy work in speeding up the work at the end of a project in order to meet production dates on the new products.

It was important to keep a project moving along briskly at every stage of its development even though some overtime might be required. A new policy was, therefore, set up stressing timing at every stage of a project, allowing more leeway in action. The policy saved a considerable amount of technical time; not only did projects move along more easily toward release dates, but technical waiting time was reduced. When a project moved along briskly, engineers seemed to keep "steamed up" on it and actually did better work. ROM improved.

Many technical departments have this chronic problem with timing of projects. Costs become excessive and projects do not meet promised dates because timing was not given emphasis at the earlier stages of a project. Time is time no matter where it occurs. To get good productivity on long-term projects, tight intermediate dates for partial accomplishment pay off.

Release on Time

At the end of a project there had been strong pressure to release designs to production in order to meet projected marketing dates; timing of the project had, therefore, been emphasized at that time. Engineers had often appeared to meet these dates by releasing designs for production that in their estimation were not complete; they had felt that the design should be sharpened more before the product itself was produced. To some extent every technical person feels this way about any project; there is always more that can be done to improve a product. But executives must pull the projects out of the laboratory when the combination of completeness of design and market acceptability seems propitious. In this case engineers had an escape hatch from the release dates, however; frequently, a week or two after engineers had released a project, they put a "hold" on the design; this action prevented any further work in production while they finished the design. In effect it nullified the release. In these cases the engineers had completed the design later and then released it. From the point of view of production, of course, the design had not been ready; they could not *produce* the product. These holds had created a great deal of expense in production and had caused substantial delays in meeting marketing dates.

Many companies do not make their engineering departments accountable for the timing impact of their design releases on the production and marketing departments. They attempt to compartmentalize product development away from production or marketing. In the process, they greatly increase the hidden costs of getting a product on the market.

To meet the hold problem in this company, the chief engineer made engineers accountable for the timing effect of late release dates on the production departments; they were held accountable for the final complete release. This final release meant no more holds; any hold extended the release dates. In effect the cost of holds was balanced against the losses of delays in release.

To give added assurance that project release dates were met, the chief engineer set a policy whereby final designs had to be approved six months before the expected production date. Any changes or holds beyond that date had to be approved by the chief engineer—an effective way to force engineers to focus their thinking on meeting dates in terms of production needs. Since engineers did not like to explain their own inability to meet release dates, they tried harder to meet them. More important, engineers were credited with meeting dates only by final complete design dates, after all holds had been completed.

SET PHASES OF A PROJECT
FOR HIGHER ROM

Even though the focus of the engineering work had now been clarified, a great deal of effort was still required in laying out the plans for the way projects were managed. The analysis now turned in that direction. One of the difficulties in planning was that all projects had been looked at as being similar whether they were new and risky projects or normal improvements of old products. In addition, there had been little differentiation made between various phases of a project. A great deal of time had often been spent on projects long after it had been clear that their potential was poor. Engineers tend to be enthusiastic about projects in which they are engaged and hate to terminate them or have them changed. To get better control, all projects were therefore set up by phases.

Feasibility Phase

All project ideas had looked promising in their beginning stages; otherwise they would not have been started. Engineers had carried some of them beyond the point, however, where it should have been clear that they could not have paid off. The chief engineer had not required a short investigative period to do some initial testing or studying to weed out projects that were not feasible for one reason or another. Projects in their beginning stages had not had the same prospects as projects which had been going on for a time and for which the objectives and approach had become clear; the risks in the former had been much greater than those in the latter. All projects had been set up as if they were final projects, however. Many that should have been scratched after a couple of weeks of preliminary investigation had gone on for months afterward with little contribution to the firm, resulting in a waste of engineering time.

The chief engineer then set up a period of several weeks during which an engineering group had the freedom to investigate the potential of a project and to prove the general idea without project approval. This was called the feasibility phase and allowed wide experimentation on the part of engineering but did not permit costly development without specific approval. The parameters were carefully defined. At a specified point of investigation the feasibility study would be reviewed by a project committee consisting of representatives of sales, manufacturing, accounting, and engineering. They would consider the project for regular project status, based on its overall business potential. Only after their approval would the project go into the next phase of development.

Concept Phase

Sometimes an apparently feasible project might have been shown to be clearly inadvisable after six or eight months of development. Too many obstacles to full development showed up. Frequently, those projects had been carried all the way through, however, even though it should have been seen earlier that the chances of success were poor. The engineers involved had been caught up by the project and had "hoped" that some new information would turn up to make the project come through; they had always been able to see something additional that they might have tried. As a consequence, considerable expense had been incurred on projects of questionable value.

To temper this laudable but costly enthusiasm, the chief engineer set up a concept phase. The purpose of this phase was to prove that the design idea proposed in the feasibility phase could be carried through for function, that is, to prove that the projected product design could be made to work profitably in a product. The concept phase would not necessarily result in a finished design, but it would result in a practical broad design that was likely to work. The project would still allow some change of direction but not of the basic plan for the design. The concept phase was tighter than the feasibility phase; it was less of a gamble.

As we indicated above, the concept phase would only begin after the project committee had approved the results of the feasibility phase and felt that the chances of success were reasonably good from a total-business point of view. Along with its approval of the concept phase of a project, the project committee would set the cost and performance targets expected as well as completion dates for the concept phase. If the committee felt it was advisable, it might authorize additional marketing or manufacturing studies before making decisions for the concept phase. No decision on final development of the project would be made, however, until after the concept phase was completed.

Final-Project Phase

At the end of the concept phase the company gave the project committee the responsibility of reviewing the results of the project to date to make sure that all aspects of the project indicated a reasonable chance of producing a profitable product. If the prospects appeared favorable, the committee would approve a final-project phase. Before making the decision, however, the project committee might require additional marketing, manufacturing, and cost data in light of the proposed design. If, after reviewing all pertinent data, it looked as though a full-blown profitable project was practical, the committee would approve a final project. Along with the approval the committee would specify the expected performance, the expected cost of the product, the estimated cost of engineering, and the date when the product should be ready for release to manufacturing. In addition, it would establish stages along the way when progress would be reviewed. Since this phase would be much closer to the final product, these stages could be set with some confidence. Overall, the project expectations in the final-project phase should be less of a gamble than in the earlier phases; the design was more likely to result in a profitable product.

ORGANIZE FOR PROFITABLE PROJECTS

A plan for a focus on profitable results and for phases on design projects only solved part of the product development ROM. To complement it, the organization plan of the engineering department had to be further analyzed and changed to fit the changes indicated above. The purpose of any organization plan is to get a structure that will facilitate the attainment of the results expected; it should blend in with the rest of the management approach.

Get Balanced Productivity

The basic organization plan of the engineering department presented another obstacle to balanced emphasis in projects. Broadly, the department had been broken down into design engineers and production engineers. The design engineers had supposedly been responsible for designing the original components so that the vehicle would have performed as expected at a reasonable cost. The personal expectations of the design engineers differed from this objective, however; they wanted to get recognition for the excellency of their designs, not necessarily for the subsequent plant production of them. As a consequence the design engineers naturally wanted recognition only for the adequacy of their designs in meeting the requirements of the vehicle; they assumed that the production engineers, in turn, were responsible for altering the designs to fit production needs.

The production engineers often had to redesign a component so that it could be produced efficiently; designs had frequently not been practical for efficient production. There had, therefore, been conflict between the two groups. Extra time and cost had been required to resolve it to get final production designs.

The chief engineer then changed the organization plan so that the same engineering people who made the original design of a component had the responsibility for carrying all the way through a practical production design; they had to carry through on both design engineering and production engineering to make practical designs for production. In other words, the engineer who designed a component was made accountable to the point that the component could be produced efficiently in the plant. It is hard to plug engineers in and out like units for different parts of the work and expect balanced engineering work to be done. Excessive coordination is often required.

To make this new form of delegation even more productive, each engineer was made responsible for the test performance of her or his component within the vehicle. Previously, testing had been the responsibility of test engineers who were not accountable for the final component. Often, much could have been learned in testing that might have led to better design. In order to maintain balanced emphasis, the engineer was also made accountable for all the cost of the component up to the point where the component was operating effectively in a vehicle; the design was aimed at total company value for money.

Assign Work by Result

Because of the variety of skills required in designing a component, several different kinds of engineers had been involved in designing each component and several engineering departments had been involved in designing the various components of a vehicle. It had, therefore, been necessary for the engineering managers to coordinate the work of various engineers working on different parts of a component, as well as that of several engineering departments working on different components of each vehicle. They had had to informally assure the smooth tie-ins between the work of different engineers and between the work of different engineering groups in order to get workable designs. Since there had been little recognition of engineers for cooperation with each other, however, the various engineers had tended to work on their assigned segments without great concern for tie-ins with the work of others; to some extent they had usually tried to coordinate their work with that of other engineers, but they had not been responsible for doing so. The compromises that were necessary had, therefore, not always been made easily and overdesign in one specialty had not always been readily adjusted to fit the contribution of other specialties.

As part of the new overall plan each engineer was assigned a segment of achievement for a project and, wherever possible, was given the authority to plan and execute it. Every effort was made to define each segment by its contribution to a working vehicle instead of in terms of technical excellency. This contribution, in turn, was tied in to the overall project through a critical path chart and monitored on the computer to make sure that all parts came together smoothly.

Design of components had often been expensive because the work of engineers of several disciplines had had to be blended and this took engineering time. Although a component might require several disciplines—mechanical, electrical, electronics, and so forth—one discipline might have been primary to the success of the design while others were secondary. It had been the customary practice to parcel out the various parts of the design to engineers in the disciplines involved; it had seemed logical to use the highest expertise available in each discipline for each engineering problem. Presumably, this philosophy would have led to the best designs. As a consequence, a great deal of coordination of disciplines had been required. In addition, engineers in disciplines that had only a small part of the action on a particular component might have lacked interest in the project and delayed their parts, thereby delaying the whole project; their parts had not been technically exciting to them.

The system of delegation was changed so that when one major discipline was primarily required for a component with some other disciplines being secondary, the total component was given to the engineer of the major discipline, with the requirement to design all of it. In a sense, lesser expertise was being applied in the secondary disciplines. However, experienced engineers in any one discipline were usually knowledgeable to some degree in the applicable knowledge of the various other disciplines as it applied to a vehicle. In addition, they were allowed to contact the specialists in one of the other fields and demand technical help if they thought it was necessary. The gain realized by this approach to delegation occurred because engineers could then be made totally accountable for a working component and (important) have complete control over it without excessive consultation with other specialists. Because the engineers responsible for individual components would more easily make compromises of disciplines for the general good of the vehicle, very satisfactory components were then often developed at lower engineering costs and required less coordinating time and less redesign to fit the needs of the operating vehicle designed. It was, therefore, easier to meet timing requirements.

Many engineering departments suffer under the delusion that referring minor parts of a project to the disciplines concerned *always* results in better and cheaper projects; after all, the trained specialist ought to be able to do a better job. It probably goes back to the suggestion of Frederick Taylor, the father of scientific management, to break down all work into specialized parts for greater productivity. The reasoning is fallacious, however. Specialists may give a project little consideration if their parts are minor; they may develop overblown specialized analyses on projects that require only reasonable attention. Besides this, they resist compromise with other specialists for the good of the total project. Coordination between disciplines is, therefore, made more difficult.

Head Counting Is Not Personnel Control

One of the problems that had occurred in project cost control had developed because the budgets of engineering managers (and, therefore, of their subordinates) had been based on numbers of people. Engineering managers had been given a total budgeted number of people, whether or not their approved technical projects required that number. They, in turn, had then assigned their engineers to their engineering supervisors. There had been a natural tendency for engineering supervisors to try to keep all their people, whether or not the section was overstaffed (trained, competent engineers were valuable if you were later assigned a demanding project). All the supervisors had wanted to keep their skilled people. As a consequence of this head-count budgeting, engineers had often been working on unauthorized projects; the engineering supervisors had argued that they had to do this to get projects done because project approvals had been too slow. They had further argued that most of the projects would have later been approved anyway—a questionable argument. The practice had frequently led to extra engineering costs and to frustration if the projects had later been rejected after a great deal of time had been applied to them.

A new approach was instituted so that personnel budgets were determined by approved project requirements. In addition, project approvals were speeded up by the project committee. Engineering supervisors were then held accountable for costs against budgets of approved projects. Further, a policy was established that all costs had to be assigned to a project. The setup encouraged engineering supervisors to keep their complements closer to what was needed for their approved projects. It also made sure that most engineering time was used for approved projects.

Supervise for More ROM

As in most large engineering departments, projects had varied in their requirements for specific engineering skills. The engineering department had, therefore, found it understandably hard to assign engineers to one engineering supervisor permanently and thereby get a continuity of supervision. Instead, it had been customary to assign a variety of engineering specialists from different disciplines to the various engineering supervisors of the individual projects when they had been needed. When engineers had no longer been needed on a project, they had been assigned to another engineering supervisor. Engineers had, therefore, been assigned to engineering supervisors temporarily, and often on a part-time basis, instead of on a permanent and full-time basis. The practice had seemed logical because the projects on which they had worked only needed certain disciplines temporarily or on a part-time basis. As a consequence of the practice, engineering supervisors had not felt responsible for the training and development of the people temporarily assigned to them nor for the balanced accomplishment of these engineers. On the other hand, specialist managers had not felt committed to the projects because their engineers were assigned to engineering supervisors reporting to other managers for supervision on the projects. The feeling was strengthened because, in many cases, their specialties were only minor (though necessary) parts of the projects.

The assignment method was changed so that engineering supervisors would have the same engineers assigned to them on a continuous basis, as much as possible. On the other side, to help make these assignments work, projects were partly laid out by the complements under the various engineering supervisors. At first blush this kind of assignment of engineers seems impossible in an engineering department, considering the variability in projects; projects are different in their requirements of different combinations of disciplines. In practice, however, it is extraordinary how frequently you can assign engineers to an individual engineering supervisor permanently and work out projects accordingly. When it can be done, projects can usually be managed with higher engineering accomplishment.

One of the causes of longer project time had been the length of time taken to train new engineers in the special company requirements. There had been an assumption that professional engineers did not need much training; after all, they were college-trained professionals. This conception was not true; engineers had usually needed substantial training in the company's accumulated expertise and its practices in order to be fully productive. They had needed training in the application of their technical knowledge to the problems peculiar to the company.

One of the reasons that it often takes an excessively long time for young engineers to be able to make a full contribution in many companies is that supervisors do not train engineers. They have not even been taught *how* to train, either in college or in the company. In this engineering department, the engineering supervisors were taught how to train engineers and also encouraged to assume the training responsibility because of the new permanent assignment of engineers.

Because both engineering supervisors and engineers were now made accountable for projects all the way through to production practicality, they could be given a greater part in the planning and release of the projects; they were now committed to completion dates. Engineering supervisors were brought in to help establish performance objectives for projects along with appropriate time and cost targets. This broadening of responsibility allowed more decentralization of decisions to individual engineers and secured a greater commitment to project objectives on the part of the engineering supervisors.

Maintaining a Product Line Is Different from New Development

The firm had successfully built a strong product line over the past years. In doing so heavy emphasis had been placed on developing new additions to fill out the line; it is more effective in the marketplace to have a full line of products. Some engineers were still operating as if they were building a line, however, instead of simply keeping it up; it is hard for people to change a direction of long standing. But conditions had changed. The product line had been established. All that had then been needed had been the updating of the line—the improvements that would keep the line's position in the market.

In order to meet the required change in emphasis, a new approval system was put in that limited the time spent on existing models to needed changes only; and model changes were only activated as needed. Only products that were clearly new were set up as full developmental projects; they were then given more attention.

Many engineering departments go through a period when they are building a product line; it usually occurs in the initial, heavy-growth stage of the business. But then the situation changes when the product line is well developed and the principal emphasis should be placed on the maintenance of the line and on the upgrading required to be competitive. Ordinarily, a different form of operation is required, or excessive costs result.

Components had often been designed in engineering departments at different locations and each produced in a plant near where it was designed. The design and production of a component had thereby been carried out in one location. Presumably, the relationship between engineering and production had, therefore, been improved. A great deal of coordination had been required, however, to tie the various engineering segments of components together to make a good vehicle. Constant consultations had been required between design engineers and between engineering departments on both the component design and the integral system of the vehicle. Many times, one engineering department had not quite met the timing or technical requirements of another and so delayed the other department. At other times, a department had overdone its portion of a design, so the design had to be scaled back, or else one otherwise good component would not mesh well with another in a vehicle.

In order to coordinate all the parts of a project, a project manager was set up to control it. Although specialists had a tendency to go off on well-intentioned tangents in their specialties, the project manager would make sure that their efforts blended with the work of other specialists, that they were effective collectively. Project managers would, therefore, control the total funds for a project no matter which engineering departments spent them. In addition, project managers would make final decisions on costs and on integrating design control; the project manager would have the authority to pull individual parts of a project back in light of the total project needs as they developed to make sure that all parts were tied together technically and that necessary timing requirements would be met. The project manager facilitated compromise between disciplines and between engineering departments in order to attain more effective vehicles for the cost from the projects.

In order to make a project manager effective, project cost figures had to be put together in detail early so that decisions could be made promptly; previously, cost data had often been compiled too late for constructive action or had lacked some breakdowns that had been needed to make sound decisions. In one simple case the change to the new procedure saved an estimating error of $1½ million by compiling data on the problem early on a worldwide basis.

PROTOTYPES CAN AID A PROJECT

Some of the timing problems of projects had stemmed from the building of experimental models. The analysis now reviewed these problems. They often had occurred in this way. While designing a component, a design engineer had often needed some experimental item tested before going ahead. Since the testing had been done by test engineers, design engineers had to wait their turn on their projects to fit the schedule of the test engineers. While waiting, they had not done as much engineering work as they might have. It had been hard for design engineers to enthusiastically work productively at other fill-in work; they had been so immersed in their current project that it had been hard to dive energetically into other temporary work. In addition, the testing had not always given the design engineer the information that was wanted. For example, the design engineer may have merely wanted to prove an idea, but the test engineer may have wanted to do other, in-depth testing to suit a sense of professional excellence. The extra testing would have taken more time, however.

Testing procedure was changed so that testing was made part of the personal job of the design engineers. They could then control their own testing and direct it toward information they needed when they needed it.

When the final prototype of the complete vehicle had been built, other problems had occurred. It had seemed economical to have many of the prototype parts produced right in the production department; after all, production people were skilled in doing this work and had the machines that were needed. Besides, it had been reasoned, production departments would become familiar with the new parts, knowledge which would be helpful when the product went into production. The critical point that had been missed was that the requirements for the building of a part for a prototype had been different from those for production vehicles; building a prototype had not been the same as building a vehicle in regular production. The objective in a prototype should have been to prove that the extremes in tolerances were sound. Only then would the engineer have been assured that production could safely use these limits.

Frequently, the reason products of companies fail is that, using the same rationale as this company, the parts for prototypes are made by the production department to be within engineering specification limits. It seems logical because production people are skilled in production. In production, however, they are not trying to prove the "permissible extremes"; proving extremes of tolerances is not a normal production problem.

To correct this prototype problem, a prototype shop was set up separately from production, equipped with extra machines and staffed with highly specialized machine operators. The prototype shop then produced most of the prototype parts according to the needs of engineering. The prototype shop was made part of the engineering department in order to keep it close to design engineers and to keep it from being affected by production schedules or tolerances. The job of the prototype shop was to prove the practicality of the total design, or a part of it, through prototypes. It had no production responsibility and was staffed by highly skilled craftspeople dedicated to engineering's needs. They would build prototypes to prove that the design limits were practical. In practice the prototype shop also needed less time to build prototypes than the production department had needed. As part of engineering, the prototype craftspeople found that they could work with unchecked drawings because they were close to design engineers and understood their expectations; in addition, the prototype craftspeople were not bound by production deadlines. They could, therefore, speed up the testing and meet release dates better.

When the prototype parts had been made in the plant, another problem had occurred. The plant had always been pressured to meet its current customer needs; the customers had to be satisfied in order to maintain a share of the market. From the production point of view prototype components had been simply a nuisance; they required short runs and broke into customer schedules. In addition, production people had not been given extra credit for the extra time they had to spend on prototype parts (short runs and special instructions), so they had tried to put them off to the least inconvenient time possible. The waiting time might easily have been three weeks before they would have produced a prototype part. The effect had been a substantial delay in producing the prototype and, as a consequence, a postponement of the final release date since that was close to the time of prototype builds.

Much of the problem was eliminated because most of the prototype parts were now produced in the prototype shop, which, in turn, had been placed in the engineering department. For those cases where a prototype part was still made in production, a new approach was instituted focusing on engineering needs. The prototype part made in production was to be looked at as a part for a preferred customer, not for a second-rate customer as previously; it had to be rushed through correctly as quickly as possible and had to meet engineering requirements.

It was interesting to note that speed had been essential in prototype builds because the timing of prototypes had been so close to the end of an engineering project that it had a direct effect on release dates. For a prototype, it could have been worthwhile to buy a casting for twice the price you would have for production if a month or two could have been cut off delivery time of the prototype. The key had been to save time, because so much extra time and cost could have been saved later in production when the production department would have tried to meet production dates. A normal purchasing procedure of getting three competing bids could have been more costly to the company in delays than a premium price paid for quicker delivery.

This kind of time emphasis in buying required a reversal from normal purchasing philosophy: Price could be of minor importance in the overall view of the project. The buyers were then given broad price leeway in their buying if they could reduce delivery time on key items and, therefore, speed up production start-up dates on new products.

Was a management analysis of new-product development different from that of an ongoing function? The approach was similar,
but the focus was different. A major reason for the differences
was the long-range aspect of the ROM of new-product development.

Engineers were directed to customer needs, not to the "perfect
vehicle." To ensure this practical direction, sales had to secure
future application specifications. In meeting these specifications, engineers had to balance quality of the product against
cost. A key factor then developed affecting both cost and customer needs, namely, timing: from the start of even a long-term
project, timing had to be stressed right down to the release date
to production. Any reduction in project time increased potential
profit.

To get better direction, all projects were broken down into
phases. Feasibility, concept, and final-project phases encouraged
sound design and cost control. To facilitate the breakdown, the
analysis pointed out the need for an interfunctional project committee to review projects periodically and approve additional
work. To better direct the work, engineers were only allowed to
work on approved projects. It became clear that the direction
could be further sharpened by planning any of the phases
around the maintenance and improvement of the present product line rather than around the development of a new one.

The organization plan affected project effectiveness. Projects
had fewer loose ends when design and production engineering
were combined; engineers developed a stronger commitment to
the final, overall product result, a profitable product. In order to
enhance this commitment, engineers were given the responsibility for conducting their own parts tests. In addition, they were
given a complete segment of the total design, wherever possible,
so that they could trace their work to the operation of the final
product and be rewarded accordingly.

In order to get better supervision in the engineering department, more engineers were permanently assigned to each engineering supervisor; projects were broken down and assigned to
fit each engineering supervisor's complement, wherever possi-

ble. To make this organization plan work, engineering supervisors were taught to train and upgrade their engineers for greater ROM.

Project managers were set up to coordinate the project work by different engineers in different engineering sections to get the best product results. The project managers would make the compromise decisions that were needed between various engineers.

To enable everyone on a project to work well toward the final product result, good data were required on all segments of the projects. The data system on projects was, therefore, sharpened.

The prototype shop was set up in the engineering department in order to expedite the final phases of a project. The prototype shop took the responsibility for prototypes that met all the requirements of engineering. If production did make a part for a prototype, the job order would be looked upon as a job for a good customer to ensure careful attention and expedite the work. It also became clear that prototype parts had purchasing requirements that differed in quality and in timing from those of regular production parts. Prototype purchasing was, therefore, changed to place greater emphasis on timing to meet production start-up dates and on special quality requirements.

7 Bringing a New Operation Up to Expectations

Every executive in a growing company or in a new business has gone through the frustrating experience of bringing a new operation up to expectations quickly. It seems as if a whole series of "bugs" develops to prevent the operation from running smoothly. Even though the preplanning was meticulously done, the action simply does not seem to want to follow the master plan. Unanticipated problems constantly occur. While the management analysis of a new operation is similar to that of an established one, it has some special overtones that must be weighed in order to maximize ROM.

An illustration of this new operation problem was a division of a company that had built a $150 million satellite plant 20 miles away from the main plant. The operations were modernized versions of some of those in the main plant, with additional computerization. In two and one-half years production had only come up to 60 percent of the engineering predictions for the plant, however. We should point out that this firm was not a novice in the field. It had approximately 40 percent of the U.S. market in its product line, and this was an old product line that was not protected by patents. The firm had to be at least reasonably competent in its field, managerially and technologically, compared to its competitors in order to maintain its position; competition had always been ready to take away orders. The problem in the new plant was how to get production up to engineering predictions quickly. The vice president of the division decided to make an in-depth analysis of the management process in the satellite plant in order to meet this objective.

COORDINATORS ARE NOT MANAGERS

The satellite plant had been very closely allied to the main plant; many semifinished products had gone back and forth between the satellite plant and the main plant for processing before they had been shipped out. Interplant transfer of semifinished products was constant. Although the operation of the satellite was similar to that of the main plant, it was a more modern, computerized operation. It should have been more efficient when it was in full operation. Because of the close relationship with the main plant, it had seemed perfectly logical that the satellite should be set up to serve the main plant—to be an adjunct of the main plant in serving customers. This approach had, however, led to a peculiar attitude; the management people of the satellite had looked at themselves as coordinators for the main plant, instead of as managers running their own show. Following this attitude, they had operated as an extension of the management of the main plant. Decisive action on local cost problems was not being taken by the satellite managers so that excessive costs had often persisted longer than necessary.

Give Managers Freedom

How had this "coordinator" mode worked? When the satellite had problems of almost any type, satellite management had reported them, along with background information, to the management of the main plant for solution and then had reacted to whatever the management of the main plant suggested. The reporting process had been followed by all the satellite managers, from the plant manager down. In other words, they had not assumed full personal responsibility for solving their own day-to-day problems but had relied on the expertise of the main plant.

On the other hand, it had been impossible for people in the main plant to become completely familiar with the details of the current problems of the satellite. As a consequence, their advice had not always been timely or correct. They had naturally assumed that the problems of the satellite were similar to those of the main plant and missed the subtle differences of the satellite mode of operation. Nevertheless, their advice was tantamount to an order to the satellite people.

Many companies and governmental agencies get trapped in this way when developing a new branch. The home office establishes so many controls and requirements for information in order to coordinate that the people in the individual installations do not develop as managers on their own, solving their own problems. They become accountable for activity—informing and carrying out main-office instructions—instead of for accomplishment. The new operation has difficulty operating on its own. The pressure on branch people does not encourage it.

To correct this coordinator problem, the relationship of the satellite was changed so that it would operate as if it were an independent plant 2000 miles away, with full responsibility for getting results from the satellite, not merely for informing people in the main plant. From the plant manager down, the responsibility of each manager was redefined in terms of getting accomplishment; the coordination with the main plant was related to this responsibility. This accomplishment, in turn, was formalized into balanced objectives for each management position down through the foremen, and the recognition system (pay, appraisals, etc.) was changed accordingly. The rule of completed, delegated work was installed in order to broaden the sense of responsibility; under this rule managers were made accountable for the accomplishment expected of them in the period, no matter who helped them or who was informed. Getting help from higher managers after informing them does not change this responsibility. In the satellite, managers were made accountable for accomplishment in their areas whether or not they informed the main plant about a problem. It was their problem to solve; the net accomplishment was their responsibility.

Assistants Are Expensive

But these changes corrected only part of the problem. The analysis had to go deeper to get full ROM. Action still lagged because a system of assistant managers had been installed throughout the satellite plant. The plant manager of the satellite had an assistant plant manager; each superintendent had an assistant superintendent; in many cases, general foremen had assistant general foremen. These assistants had been appointed for good, logical reasons. In some cases the assistants had been appointed simply to help the superiors carry through on their many responsibilities. In other cases the rationale that had been applied was that the assistant would fill in some part of the needed background lacking in the manager; management had wanted to make sure that every problem got adequate attention, so the manager was "shored up" with an assistant who had the skills the manager lacked. In addition, the assistant position had been looked upon as a good way to train a backup for the manager. Presumably, the assistant would have been exposed to all aspects of the superior's position.

Many companies mistakenly follow the assistant mode of operation, feeling that it is good training for future managers. On the contrary, it is poor training. A future manager is strengthened most by being made accountable for accomplishment, not by helping a superior and simply being exposed to problems. Assistant managers who are set up in the position of generally helping a manager, or else simply coordinating, may actually be weakened. They are not accountable for accomplishment but suffer under an illusion of accountability by being involved in many problems.

The assistant-manager approach had actually reinforced the coordinator attitude among the satellite managers; the assistants had developed into kinds of coordinators for the managers. On the other hand, the coordinator relationship with the main plant had encouraged the assistant setup; extra follow-up of main-office decisions had taken a great deal of time of the managers so that the assistants had seemed necessary. The assistant setup had also reinforced the activity emphasis; it had encouraged a great many meetings so that everybody could be informed. Both the managers and the assistant managers had been at most of the production meetings in both the main plant and the satellite plant; all had to know what was going on. But the meetings, in turn, had further decreased the sense of personal accountability for results of the assistants. After all, if something went wrong with a decision, "Everybody had agreed, therefore you can't blame me."

This overemphasis on participation per se has weakened many operations; participation becomes an end in itself rather than a way to get more results. Participation can be helpful if it is required for accomplishment, is directed toward a result, and does not weaken a manager's sense of accountability.

In spite of the additional meeting time, the assistant-manager approach had increased communications problems by 25 percent; it had created additional levels through which decisions had to go up or down. In a sense it had created errand-person supervision; the assistants had carried information upward and downward but had not necessarily assumed responsibility for achievement. All communications are more likely to go awry when they go through additional people. Many times, both the manager and the assistant would give instructions to those below, creating confusion and frequently stalling action.

In many cases managers themselves had not felt fully accountable for problems when they had been given assistants with special expertise that the manager apparently had lacked. They had then assumed that it had been the assistants' job to solve problems involving that expertise. Since the assistants, in turn, had not felt fully accountable for accomplishment because they had not been in charge, nobody had felt accountable; a no-man's-land of accountability had developed, reducing the drive toward accomplishment.

The vice president then eliminated all the assistants so that organization structure was flattened out. Managers were trained in the specialized background that they lacked so that the absence of assistants with special expertise could not be used to rationalize lack of accomplishment. They were then expected to carry the full load. Although there was a saving in personnel cost itself, the real saving was in sparking up the management process. Management action was more incisive, accountability was not diluted, and communications improved.

REWARD MANAGERS FOR MEANINGFUL RESULTS

Though the new management plan was theoretically sound, full results were still elusive. Effectiveness was considerably reduced because, in the past, management emphasis had led to rewards for activity (for carrying out orders and for informing) not necessarily for improving company results. This emphasis had stemmed from the close interrelationship in production between the main plant and the satellite plant and had been augmented by the coordinator philosophy. The management analysis, therefore, had to turn to the management reward system.

Get Balanced Results

In a limited way there had been accountability for results. Because the plant had been new, there had been a strong emphasis on tonnage, on gross output. After all, the plant could not have hoped to be profitable if it had no product output. As the plant had gotten under way, however, the tonnage emphasis had become overdone, leading to an imbalance in results; other results like product cost, maintenance cost, and on-time delivery had not been weighed in carefully. In addition, many of these other results had been looked at as the responsibility of the specialized staff concerned, not of the line management—i.e., delivery had been the job of schedulers, maintenance had been the job of the maintenance department.

This tendency to abdicate the responsibility for part of the line work to staff is common in a complex organization. Line management often feels that accomplishment in a specialist's area is the job of the specialized staff, not of the line. After all, the staff people are the experts in the specialized fields; they should be best able to do the specialized work. The line is, therefore, absolved of the accountability for total balanced results. This thinking almost always leads to poor operation. The line must blend all specialized contributions to achieve the best overall result. Staff should be a help to line, not a replacement for it.

The first step in correcting the misemphasis on activity in the satellite was to direct the managers toward balanced results—weighing labor cost, yield, maintenance cost, and on-time shipments. A job-purpose technique was used; line management people were taught how to analyze all the results that they should be aiming at in their jobs and weigh them one against the other. Staff personnel were taught how to fit in their specialties to enhance line results. Objectives were then established in terms of these results along with weights to establish importance. Without weights there would still have been a tendency to operate as they had in the past.

Make Pay Encourage Expected Results

In light of these changes to a results emphasis, the pay system for foremen also had to be changed because it still encouraged unnecessary overtime, resulting in excessive payroll costs per unit of production. In the initial stages every effort had been made to get the plant going; overtime had been looked at with favor—anything to get the plant under way and producing. Overtime costs had seemed minor in light of this objective. The trouble was that this overtime had kept up after the plant was operating for a period of time. Overtime tends to be accepted as normal after it has been going on for a while. Many supervisors had felt that cutting overtime (and therefore the income of employees) would have led to poorer morale and, therefore, have unfavorably affected costs.

Acceptance of overtime had been strengthened because initially foremen had also been placed on an hourly basis in order to maintain differentials in pay over their hourly crew; for the same reason they had also received overtime pay. This very system had encouraged more overtime once the plant got going. It had been to the foremen's advantage to have more overtime; they themselves got more. Even though they were to be depended upon to curb overtime, it had been to their disadvantage to curb it.

The foremen were then taken off an hourly basis and placed on straight salary with no overtime. The salary assumed a few hours were necessary for planning, reports, etc. There was now no advantage to them to have extra overtime. In addition, raises of foremen were based on balanced "results" objectives, including cost per unit (and overtime was part of that cost). Foremen now had to weigh the cost of overtime versus other costs and scheduling requirements; they were encouraged to control excessive overtime costs unless there was an obvious advantage to be gained on other results.

MANAGERS MUST KNOW THEIR JOBS

But even though the managers were now made accountable for results, they still made mistakes in decisions and incurred losses because they did not fully know what their jobs were under the new setup. The problem started with the plant manager. First of all, the vice president had to redefine the plant manager's responsibility and authority from the main plant in tune with the philosophy that the plant was 2000 miles away. The plant manager was no longer primarily a coordinator. The change had to be explained both to the plant manager and to managers in the main plant. Then the plant manager had to redelegate accordingly to subordinates. Further, all satellite management had to be trained in the meaning of a managerial job in this light and encouraged to operate in this way. A major change in perspective was required.

Train to Get Higher Productivity

Since the plant was new, many first-level foremen were new to foremanship and not familiar with the work under them; they, therefore, had difficulty training their crews and adequately following up on the work. Many errors had occurred and new employees had not attained expected output. They had relied on lead people to do the training—an unreliable method; the lead people had not known how to train, and they had not always been committed to the development of a high-producing employee. In this case the foremen were, therefore, given special training in the work that they were supervising so that they could train and follow up on the work.

Many firms have the basic problem that first-level supervisors do not know the work under them well enough to train people in it and to make sure that the work is done right and efficiently. In most operations first-level supervisors must know the work that they supervise to be effective in getting high productivity from their people.

But knowing the work itself was not enough. Even though the foremen now knew the work, they still did not know how to train their new people to do this work efficiently. This training in how to train is especially critical in a new operation. The foremen were, therefore, trained in how to train so they could effectively pass on knowledge of the work.

Ever since World War II, job-instructor training (how to train) has been available as a well-developed program. This training is always effective in increasing productivity if it is applied right and proper follow-up is carried out. Even so, it is extraordinary how few companies do an adequate job of training their first-level supervisors in how to train their people. There is no other training program we know of that gives so much return for the cost. It is critical for attaining high ROM.

More Training to Get Production from Computers

In spite of the changes that were made, production on the big mill still lagged. Although the big mill was similar to other mills in the company, it was a much more computerized operation. The type of computer was new, and people in the department had not been given enough operating knowledge of the computer to fully utilize it. There had, therefore, been many operating problems, and it had seemed logical to set up a computer specialist, a staff person, to cover computer problems for all the line people. In this way, expert advice was always available for computer problems.

The computer specialist had acted as a troubleshooter, however, solving each problem, and had not acted as a trainer, passing on expertise to the line people. Since the foremen and hourly people had not been fully trained to run the computerized mill, they had been calling in the computer specialist whenever there had been a problem on any shift. The theory had been that the computer expert could best solve a computer problem. However, the process had lengthened delays and, therefore, increased downtime. In addition, more errors in production and lost time had occurred in the first place because neither the operators nor the foremen had been skilled in operating the computers on the big mill. At the same time the specialist had been run ragged solving crises twenty-four hours a day.

The plant manager changed the operation of the big mill; foremen and hourly people in the department were expected to solve more problems without calling in the specialist. To make sure that they could do this, they were trained in computer application. In order to expedite the training, some of it was done by the computer manufacturer.

Staff-line operations are frequently more efficient if the staff people give the line people all the information and knowledge possible to run their own operation. Staff should pass on its expertise to the line; it should upgrade the line. The line is then made less dependent on staff people. In most cases the best way to use specialists of any kind is to have them train other people in the use of the specialty rather than act as troubleshooters.

CAPITALIZE ON STAFF EXPERTISE

Because the management mode of operation had been directed toward the operation of the main plant, the satellite plant had not been given the full advantage of staff expertise to improve its operation. As a consequence, satellite operations often lagged. To start with, staff people of the main plant had been somewhat antagonistic to the needs of the satellite; they had looked at these needs as subordinate to those of the main plant. They had naturally felt primarily accountable for helping the main plant; after all, the latter had been a much larger operation. In tune with this thinking, they had naturally felt that the satellite should conform to their main-plant procedures instead of vice versa. Further, they had not viewed their responsibility as that of developing solutions for the specific line problems of the satellite. One consequence was a natural inclination to force the satellite to fit in with the main-plant staff schedule, which was primarily based on main-plant needs; staff had been reluctant to make the adjustments in timing or in approach that were needed to fit the satellite's requirements. As a case in point, the central computer people had been reluctant to take the extra time required to adapt programming to the needs of the satellite managers. It had been less trouble for them to use the programming already developed for the main plant.

Make Staff Improve Line Productivity

Because of the staff's view of its responsibility, the satellite had had difficulty getting specialized staff help when necessary. At other times they had difficulty getting attention for their specific problems (as against those of the main plant) as they had developed. In fairness to the main-plant staff people, they had not been encouraged to help the satellite because they had not been accountable for satellite line results; they had not been accountable for the losses in the satellite that their expertise could have prevented. They had felt that the satellite's effectiveness had been the responsibility of the satellite management. It had been their responsibility to merely provide what they felt had been appropriate advice and procedure.

It is common for the staff people in many operations to feel that the line effectiveness is not their responsibility; their responsibility ends with advising and proposing procedures. They are expert consultants. And yet there is always a line result that is the reason for the very existence of a staff person. The staff should be expected to improve that line result and, thereby, to improve line productivity in some way.

To better direct the main-plant staff people to help the line get results, they were made accountable along with the line people in the satellite for the results on which their staff expertise impinged; both groups were then rewarded if these results were achieved. If the line got a better result in a staff area, the latter would also get recognition for it; if the line did not get a result, the staff that was supposed to influence that result would also suffer. They were, therefore, encouraged to work together toward better line results down to the first-line level in the satellite, where results would finally be evidenced.

Decentralize to Increase ROM

Part of the difficulty in getting good staff service for the problems of the satellite had occurred because the main-plant staff supervisors and many of the staff people were at the main plant 20 miles away. In theory, even though they had been physically removed from the satellite, their higher professional expertise should have allowed them to serve the satellite better. The problem was that even though they were only 20 miles away, they had not had an intimate knowledge of the problems of the satellite. In addition, they had been looked at as main-plant staff and, therefore, had allegiance there; their primary responsibility had been with the main plant.

The vice president then changed the main-plant staff organization. Wherever possible, staff people were decentralized to report directly to the satellite. Industrial engineering people working for the satellite were put under the plant manager of the satellite; plant engineering and maintenance for the satellite were also changed to report directly to the plant manager of the satellite. Previously, the maintenance people had been physically located at the satellite but had still reported to the main-plant maintenance department. While this location had been helpful, it had not been the same as reporting to the satellite plant manager; since they had been directed by the main-plant maintenance department, they had naturally followed main-plant procedures and priorities, which may not have suited the needs of the satellite.

After maintenance was placed under the plant manager of

the satellite, it was decentralized still further to get it closer to the actual maintenance problems. Each individual superintendent was given a maintenance crew to serve that department; maintenance people were thereby tied into the production section that they served. They were made part of the production team under the superintendent to help maximize production.

In effect, a modular form of organization was developed having staff report as low as possible in the line organization of the satellite. Even where the staff function could not be decentralized to the satellite, the situation was approximated by allowing satellite management to make the decisions in the function; in other words, decision making was decentralized. At the same time the vice president made the plant manager accountable for the cost of carrying through on the staff work that was requested and for any impact of the work on the productivity of the satellite.

Make Central Staff Serve the Satellite

As we pointed out earlier, even though the satellite plant was only 20 miles away and, productionwise, essentially part of the main plant, it had to be looked at as independent in order to get maximum ROM in the satellite. In analyzing this relationship more deeply, it became clear that when this change in viewpoint was affected, the staff of the main plant now had to assume two different types of responsibility. On the one hand, the staff people continued to give local staff service to the main plant like any plant staff group; on the other hand, they had to take a different perspective when serving the satellite management. They had to act as a central staff to the satellite. They then had a greater responsibility to train people in the satellite—to pass their expertise on to help the satellite solve its own problems. In order to keep the satellite staff slim, the main-plant staff was also made responsible for providing the satellite with extra people in the specialties in tight periods; the main-plant staff kept the overload crews. This function was especially critical in maintenance, for example.

To make it advantageous for main-plant staff people to help

the satellite, they were made accountable for the total accomplishment of their functions in terms of results in the satellite; significantly, they would be accountable for these results even though they might not supervise the people directly. They had a functional relationship to the satellite staff.

In order to capitalize on a staff function in any operation, the so-called functional relationship—a dotted-line relationship—must always imply accountability for the effect on line productivity even though the functional department does not have a direct control of line people. That is the nature of a staff relationship. Otherwise, staff grows excessively and staff work is less helpful to the line.

Make Information a Stimulating Tool

As we stated earlier, the information system had been inadequate for the satellite's requirements; it had not promptly pointed out where management action was needed in the satellite. As a consequence, some decisions lagged. Many of the records had not suited the needs of the satellite because they had been geared to the problems of the main plant. Since the records had focused on the problems of the main plant, they, too, had subtly encouraged the coordinator approach; they further encouraged main-plant control. At the same time satellite managers had seldom received current or daily information on their own operations to help them make prompt operational decisions. Records had not been geared to the satellite's specific problems because they had been set up by people in the main plant who, of course, had not been close to satellite problems. They had assumed that the record approach which had been developed to service the main plant would also fit the day-to-day satellite production which had been scheduled.

Why had current records been so important to productivity? The satellite had been essentially a job shop operation where each order could have distinctive characteristics and requirements. Production needs could have changed frequently. There had, however, been inadequate cost data by order, by department, and by section to help the satellite detect a problem quickly, solve it, and make quick changes in operation. In addition, significant data had not been collated so that staff people could be informed of the effect of their functions and be made accountable for it. Since staff had been accountable by its activity anyway, there had seemed no need for this information.

In order to better capitalize on records to increase satellite ROM, decision making on setting up the data system was changed so that the satellite made decisions wherever possible on what information was needed; decision making on records was partly decentralized. It was then the obligation of the data processing people to provide this information as directed. In order to maintain perspective, however, the cost of the records had to be charged against the satellite. Later, a small computer would be placed in the satellite to do most of the information work there. In order to better encourage staff functions to help the line, cost data were assembled to reflect the subresults on which staff people should have an impact. They could then better utilize their expertise to help the line.

Schedule for Productivity

Delays and poor utilization of equipment occurred because of the way production had been scheduled. Because the departments of the satellite had been closely integrated with the departments of the main plant, central scheduling control had been a necessity. The processes of the various departments of the satellite had been closely interrelated and, in addition, closely related to those of the main plant; goods-in-process had gone back and forth between the departments of both plants for further processing. In order to optimize production in all departments and also meet shipping dates to customers, some scheduling had to be done in a central scheduling department. The work of the various production departments had to be integrated.

The scheduling department had carried out its scheduling responsibility by assigning a portion of the scheduling work to each person in the scheduling department; assignments had not been based on responsibility for an order or for the efficiency of a particular operating department. The effect of this organization plan had been to fragment the scheduling of an order so that more coordination was required, leading to less efficiency in production. There had been little accountability of scheduling people for production cost resulting from misscheduling. Schedulers had not been tied closely to the results that they had affected in the satellite plant (or the main plant, for that matter).

As a consequence of the scheduling mode of operation, overall scheduling of orders had only been tied together by meetings with the scheduling manager; this person alone had to coordinate all the work through departmental meetings of scheduling people, since there were many orders and many departments involved in each order. These meetings had resulted in quite a bottleneck because the scheduling manager had to make most of the decisions. In addition, the process had been antagonistic to the development of a decision-making scheduling staff.

The scheduling operation was then changed so that scheduling work was combined by order; as far as possible, each scheduling person was made responsible for an order straight through production to get that order produced efficiently and on schedule. The change ensured that goods-in-process were available when needed for further processing in the next department. In addition, all the scheduling work in both plants was then tied together by the scheduling manager to get optimum efficiency in all operating departments, i.e., to get similar runs together in each department to cut down changeovers.

To make the new scheduling plan work, accountability in the scheduling department was also changed; it was based on the effect of good scheduling on the various operating departments, both in the main plant and in the satellite—on availability of goods-in-process for the next department, on the length of runs (productivity), and on delivery dates. When the plan was fully put into effect, the scheduling staff was cut by a third and was still doing a better job of efficiently scheduling the various operations.

A NEW OPERATION NEEDS A CHANGE IN THINKING

What was critical in getting higher ROM in a new operation? Although production in the satellite was closely related to that in the main plant, the satellite was best analyzed as an entity in itself. So it was decided that the satellite should operate as if it were 2000 miles away. It became apparent as the analysis progressed that if the satellite was to operate efficiently, the umbilical cord to the main plant had to be cut; a new relationship with the main plant had to be developed.

The management structure of the satellite was changed to accommodate the changed status of the satellite. Assistant managers were eliminated, and managers ran their operations more firmly. They were no longer accountable for simply informing the main plant; they stopped being coordinators. The rewards for managers were then based on balanced results achieved. Overtime for foremen (which had encouraged more overtime for the crews) was also eliminated.

Since the satellite was a new plant, there were a number of training problems which had to be met. All managers were trained in the meaning of responsible management. First-level supervisors were trained in the work of their subordinates and in how to train so that they could get new people up to high productivity quickly. More specifically, the operators and the foremen of the big mill were trained to run its computer operation without heavy reliance on staff computer experts.

Staff was changed to serve the satellite. First, direct maintenance, industrial engineering, and plant engineering were decentralized to the satellite plant manager for better tie-in with satellite line people. Second, main-plant staff people were made accountable for all the line results that they affected. Third, they were required to pass on their expertise to people in the satellite so that it could operate as independently as possible.

Central scheduling was reorganized by customer order to plan production for the satellite better. Along with this change, scheduling people were made accountable by order both for their effect on satellite plant costs and for timeliness of shipments.

The information system was also changed to serve the satellite's special needs; it was set up to help satellite management make prompt decisions in all departments. The data were, therefore, revised to reflect progress of each order through the plant. In order to utilize staff expertise better, data were also accumulated to reflect the contribution of staff people to line results.

What was realized through this management analysis of the ROM of a new operation? Within a year all three departments of the satellite were up to expectations; one was 15 percent above it, another 60 percent above. In total, profit contribution of the satellite was increased $25 million per year.

8 Improving Regional ROM

It is always difficult to direct operations from a distance; it is hard to get complete information on day-to-day problems. It is, therefore, hard to keep control and, at the same time, stimulate incisive local action. The problems are multiplied in a fast-moving business that is changing almost daily.

A good example was a region of the marketing department of an oil company. The region had about 100 sales representatives and was considered a well-run region. In addition, the marketing department itself was well respected in the industry—a real tribute since it was a very competitive industry. The problem posed was, How can the regional contribution to profit be increased even more? Chapter 8 describes the way the four-step method of management analysis was applied to the problem.

MAKE THE DEALER SUCCESSFUL

As in most oil companies, most of the final sales to the users had been made through independent dealers. The company had sold a variety of products directly to the dealers; the dealers had been the direct customers on the books of the company. They, in turn, had then resold products to the final consumers. It had been natural to look at the dealers as the customers. After all, they had purchased the products from the company; they had been billed for these products. The customer relationship of the dealers had been fortified by the fact that legally they had been independent. The consequence of the setup had been that sales had been missed because the dealers had not been looked at by management as the bottom of the marketing chain of the company. Policies and procedures reflected this viewpoint.

When firms sell through secondary distribution (dealers or distributors), it is a common management error to forget that, in practice, the final customers of the company are the ultimate consumers of the products. If the company is to be effective, the primary marketing effort should focus on the consumers, not on the dealers or distributors. Management must look at the dealers or distributors as part of the company marketing team. They should be sold *through,* not *to.*

Because of the independence of the dealers in this company, most of the management systems had been based on the premise that it was the job of the sales representative to sell products to the dealers; marketing programs and rewards had been aimed at selling products for the inventories of the dealers. The approach had seemed logical; if the dealers had substantial inventories of all the products, they would try to sell the products to get rid of the inventories and then reorder. After all, they had their own money invested and should have wanted to sell the products in their inventories in order to recover their investments. They would presumably then buy more.

However, because of sales pressure on them from the company, dealers might have had their money invested in the wrong inventory to fit the demands of their customers; areas might vary in customer demand from the pattern expected under the various product-promotion programs. Dealers had not, therefore, always had the money to buy other items that had been needed to satisfy customer needs. In addition, because of the large inventory investment that had been built up as a result of the promotion programs, some dealers had been short of money to employ and pay competent employees. As a consequence, they had been giving poor service to customers although consumer sales had depended on good service. In essence then, the sales representatives had been pushed to get dealers to buy but had not been encouraged to emphasize dealer success. Merchandising through dealers had not been the prime responsibility of sales representatives.

Program Success Is Not Sales Success

The dealer marketing philosophy had naturally led to an emphasis on sales program accountability—maximum sales to dealers during the period of a program on the particular products pushed. How had the programs worked? Special programs and contests had been run at different times during the year to push sales of individual products. Almost all these programs had been short-term programs, lasting only one or two months; there had been comparatively little home-office emphasis on the product concerned during the rest of the year. As a consequence there were fewer sales made during the rest of the year.

Most field salespeople had felt that the broad marketing thinking behind each program was sound. The programs had been national, however, and had not accounted for territorial differences; a product marketing program might have pushed the wrong items for a territory—or pushed them at the wrong time. Customers of the dealers had not always followed the programs in their buying patterns: They had often wanted to buy a product at a different time of the year.

Sales representatives had naturally wanted to look good on each program; after all, the results were tabulated and highly visible in the home office. The sales representatives had, therefore, often tried to save up certain product sales for the program time. In the process, they had sometimes lost some sales; consumers might have needed the product at a different time and might, therefore, have purchased from a competitor. More fundamentally, the program system had not pushed the sales representatives to train the dealers in customer service and in merchandising so that they, in turn, could have trained the attendants who dealt with the consumer; in the long run the attendants were the primary sales contact with the final consumer.

Emphasize the Final Sale

The vice president of sales decided that a basic change in marketing philosophy was needed which would emphasize the final sale to the consumer. The job of the sales representatives was redefined as that of selling *through* the dealer, not *to* the dealer. They were made accountable for dealer results; their basic job was to make the dealer successful. They, therefore, were to concentrate on those things that would fit each dealer's needs, not on simply carrying out the home-office programs through the dealer. This approach automatically considered the special differences between territories.

To make this "dealer-success" approach work, however, the accountability system for sales representatives and sales supervisors had to be changed. Instead of being held accountable for spot successes on each of the short-range sales programs, they were evaluated on their total yearly accomplishment on all products against the current potential for their territories.

The previous management practices based on programs still presented an accountability problem, however. In the past a tabulation had been compiled in the home office indicating how well each sales representative and sales supervisor had done on each program; each person had been ranked against the others. Presumably, competition between them would act as an incentive. Naturally, no sales representative or sales supervisor wanted to be low on this highly visible list. So, even though the adoption of the programs in particular territories had always been theoretically voluntary, these lists had, in effect, made the programs compulsory; even if a program had not fit a particular territory or area, no one had felt that it would be politic to ignore it.

The home-office lists of achievement on each program were then eliminated, and the programs were made truly voluntary. Emphasis was placed on total balanced sales for the year and could vary with the characteristics of the territories. Local salespeople could then use the programs that best fit the needs of each territory. There was no special pressure to adopt a program that did not fit a territory.

Need Merchandising, Not Selling

But how could sales representatives make their dealers successful? The primary way was by teaching dealers better methods of merchandising products to the consumers and by encouraging dealers to apply good merchandising techniques. The importance of field merchandising had been well recognized by the firm; field merchandising meant getting the dealer to sell products to consumers. In an experiment, several field merchandisers had been set up to work intensively with a few dealers to teach them better merchandising methods. The program had been effective in helping the dealers get sales; it had, therefore, proved the value of merchandising. The difficulty with the operation of the field merchandisers was that they had undercut the sales representatives assigned to service the dealers. The field merchandisers had worked with the same dealers as had some of the sales representatives; since the field merchandisers had been helping the dealers merchandise, the dealers had begun to look to them for help on any problem. The sales representatives had been bypassed.

The field merchandiser setup was eliminated. Instead, merchandising was made a prime responsibility of the sales representatives, and they were made accountable for annual throughput to consumers, not simply for special program sales to dealers. They were now expected to train their own dealers to merchandise. The field merchandisers, in turn, were used more broadly as regional staff people to train the sales representatives and sales supervisors in merchandising; the field merchandisers were expected to pass on their expertise so that field salespeople could train their own dealers to merchandise. The result was a broader use of the field merchandising technique and a more productive utilization of the sales representatives.

But training the sales representatives in merchandising was not enough. Even though they had now learned merchandising techniques to improve their dealers, they did not necessarily know how to effectively transmit the techniques to the dealers. The sales representatives were, therefore, given special training on how to train the dealers and the attendants in the application of each merchandising technique so that it was effective with consumers. In addition, the school for new dealers was changed accordingly so that dealers were taught how to teach the merchandising techniques to their attendants in the first place. Beyond this, the dealers' school was broadened to give dealers more knowledge of business management in order to make dealers more successful financially.

To make the new merchandising program effective, the regional staff was trained to put its new merchandising programs into training form so that both sales representatives and sales supervisors could use them effectively in training the dealers. Staff expertise could then be more effectively translated into field results. Once this overall change of emphasis was installed (from program concentration to overall dealer effectiveness), a number of regional staff people were no longer needed; the local line people could carry out the grass-roots merchandising work without them. Any additional regional staff people beyond that merely sapped field time to inform the staff without a commensurate return in the field.

A Sales Supervisor Is a Trainer

Even with these changes, the sales representatives could not continue to carry through completely because they were not being trained directly by the sales supervisors in all the changing merchandising methods and in other ways that were being developed to make dealers successful. The problem centered on the sales supervisors; although their responsibility to train their sales representatives was stated in their job description, they had acted primarily as senior salespersons, not as trainers. The sales supervisor had acted as a troubleshooter who had gone to a dealer with a sales representative when a difficult problem had occurred. The supervisor had then worked with the dealer, solved the problem, and said to the sales representative, "See, that's the way to do it." This method had been natural for sales supervisors because they had been promoted on the basis of their ability to work with dealers.

But watching is a poor method of training; the sales representatives had not learned well in the process. In effect, training had been downgraded by the process, even though the requirement to train sales representatives had been carefully pointed out in the job description of the sales supervisors. The fact that the training responsibility had been in their job description had made little difference because the sales supervisors had not been taught how to train sales representatives in these methods.

Sales supervisors were then taught how to train so that they could upgrade their sales representatives on the application of these methods. The vice president of sales also made it clear that training sales representatives was their primary responsibility.

Many companies erroneously assume that because a responsibility is stated in the job description, people are carrying it out whether they have been trained to do it or not. "It ain't necessarily so." Unless people know how to carry out the responsibility and, in addition, unless executive weight is placed upon it, little may be done on it.

You've Got to Have Time

Even though all these changes were effected, there was still a problem of time that prevented full implementation of the new approach. It occurred because of the carry-over of past practice. In fairness to the sales representatives, they had not had enough time to spend with the dealers to train them in merchandising even if encouraged to do so. Why? Because, at the request of staff people, they had been spending a great deal of time getting information from the field to help staff develop its programs. In addition, the staff programs themselves required considerable time to implement. The firm had drifted into a "going there anyway" philosophy; the sales representatives could presumably carry out all these extra duties without any loss because they were in the territories anyway. But every extra activity required of the sales representatives had taken time away from that available to do other work with the dealers. Field people had been spending much of their time helping central staff instead of central staff doing what it should to help the field people be more effective with their time in working with the dealers.

This whole time problem had been magnified because there had been as many as twenty-five programs going on during a year. Beyond this, the staff requests had often had short fuses; the staff had frequently wanted information right away whether or not it was convenient for the sales representative. In addition, the weight of the executive office had been behind the staff. As a consequence, the sales representatives had to drop everything to get information for the staff people quickly. They, therefore, had even less time for their regular work with dealers and naturally looked at that work as less important.

This time problem of the field is common in many large, centralized staff operations. Each overall staff activity seems so worthwhile that executives overlook the drain on field time. But, in the last analysis, it is usually the wise application of this field time that will determine the success of the implementation of good staff programs.

The vice president of sales changed the staff information system so that when the sales supervisors were given a request by a staff person, they would give an estimate of the time of the sales representatives required to satisfy the request and, in addition, of the applicability of the projected staff program to their territories. The burden of proof was then placed on the staff people to show that the expected return from the program justified the cost of acceding to their information requests. The pressure was on them to make sure that satisfactory line results ensued from the programs.

This principle of making staff justify all the lost time that it causes should apply wherever you have staff—the burden of proof should be on staff to show that all the work and trouble it causes the line are worthwhile in helping the line get more results. In other words, staff should be expected to show increased line results that justify staff demands. Otherwise, staff work can easily wind up making a net negative contribution to the organization.

To effect the new approach, the vice president of sales broadened the responsibility and the authority of the regional staff.

Regional staff was set up to *screen* home-office programs and cut them out if they were not applicable to a particular area in the region. Previously, the regional staff had viewed its responsibility as primarily that of pushing through home-office programs to get them in. That is what executive pressure had seemed to indicate. As a consequence, programs had often been pushed even in territories where the conditions made application inappropriate at the time. Strangely enough, this narrow view of the job of regional staff leads to rigidity and poor results from skilled home-office staff people. In application their work may actually lead to less corporate accomplishment.

As a consequence of all the changes that resulted from the analysis of the management climate, sales supervisors could now carry more responsibility; sales representatives were more effective and had more time to spend with dealers. The district managers' span of management could then be broadened since sales supervisors were carrying more of the load. Later, three district offices could, therefore, be eliminated and their functions folded under the remaining district managers.

IMPROVE PROFIT MARGINS

The next step of the analysis focused on profit potential. It examined ways to improve profit margins without unduly affecting sales volume. Since the emphasis in the sales department had been on sales to dealers, especially through promotion programs, profit margins had not been emphasized at the field level; it was assumed that optimum profit margins would result from sales to dealers with the prices set by a home-office price expert. The field presumably had little effect on margins.

Territories Are Different

One stumbling block to profit maximization had been the tendency to treat all sales representatives and sales supervisors the same. Their problems had been looked upon as similar to those of others at their level; uniform profit decisions could, therefore, be made by the home office for all. Sales representatives had not been free to solve the unique profit problems of their particular territories or areas. The job descriptions had been the same; objectives had been similar for all jobs that seemed to have had the same title, even though there may have been differences in local problems that had to be addressed. In effect, the objectives had not, therefore, highlighted the specific opportunities that arose in each particular job.

For example, one territory might have had three stations without dealers in place; the prime way the sales representative could have increased profit contribution was to have obtained three good dealers quickly. Another territory might have had a full dealer complement but had two superstations just go on stream in the last year. The main job of the sales representative should have been to get them up to speed. For best results the objectives of the two sales representatives should have been different. The sales representative in the first territory should have stressed recruitment of new dealers, while the one in the second territory should have upgraded the merchandising and service of the superstations to make them profitable.

This uniformity of objectives for similar jobs is common to many MBO programs and is often a reason for disappointing results. Specific objectives should be based on the opportunities and problems in the particular job in this period.

The vice president of sales changed the MBO system throughout the department to emphasize the special contribution of each person. All the field people were put through job-purpose procedure to focus each person on what had to be accomplished in each particular job in the particular period; the procedure focused on the variations in local territory conditions that had to be met in order to maximize profit contribution. Objectives for sales representatives were set accordingly; local people were then freer to meet their particular local problems.

Regional staff people were also put through the job-purpose procedure with the emphasis directing them toward field results; their objectives were then stated in terms of field requirements so that they were in tune with the sales representatives. In this way they were encouraged to help local field people effectively meet their objectives; staff would try to push the best profit approach for each territory and assist the sales representatives instead of simply pushing their specialties.

Volume Does Not Mean Profit

Past accountability systems had concentrated on sales volume to the dealer, not necessarily profitable volume as such. It had been assumed that increased profit would develop through increased volume to the dealer and through carrying out the programs developed by the home office; the dealer would naturally try to sell off inventory and then reorder. To some extent this assumption was valid but only partially so.

Many sales departments focus practically all their attention on sales volume, under the supposition that increased volume will automatically maximize profit. It rarely does. Other factors almost always come into play so that other emphasis is also needed.

The home-office merchandising programs of this company, while often effective, had not by themselves been suited to the best profit contribution from each district or territory; the opportunities were not the same. The rankings on programs had not allowed each district to focus on its best profit contribution; as in most home-office programs, they worked toward uniformity and, therefore, away from specific differences in territories. Minor-profit items in an area had often been given just as much emphasis as high-profit items because there was a home-office ranking on each program. Minor products, therefore, tended to get the same emphasis as major products. Major products had not received the extra time they deserved, since there had been a limit to the time that each sales representative had available. In addition, the programs had not emphasized dealer success or service to the customers of the territory to build profitably for the future. They were not flexible enough in application. These reasons underscored the elimination of the home-office rankings on programs mentioned earlier.

Make District Managers Profit Managers

Could the district managers, fundamentally sales managers, be made accountable for profit? After all, most of their training and experience had been in sales and marketing, not in business generally. This proposition had been studied by the home office for some time, and it had seemed almost impossible to develop a suitable profit measurement because of all the overhead, refining, and production costs that had entered into the cost picture —costs that were not affected by district managers. In addition, many cost and price decisions for programs had been made in either the regional office or the home office. It had not, therefore, seemed fair to hold them accountable for profit.

In order to get around the objections to district manager profit accountability, the vice president of sales had a performance index developed which indicated the district contribution to profit; it excluded overhead and headquarters costs, terminal costs, refinery charges, taxes, and so on—items over which the district managers had little control. The purpose was to encourage district managers to take a realistic view of district volume and profit together, in other words, to achieve a balanced operation in the district.

The company then found that creative district managers could affect profit in a number of ways. For example, after the performance index was installed, one district manager turned down 9 million gallons of less profitable gasoline sales in order to concentrate on other, more profitable sales—an action almost unprecedented in the sales department.

Many executives despair of profit measurements for managers because the managers have little control of some of the factors. In fact, full profit measurements may direct managers to give too much attention to factors on which they can have little impact. In many operations complete profit measurements are not necessary to direct people toward their maximum profit contribution. Simply use a measurement that encourages them to make the contribution they can; you are interested in the return they can contribute.

District Sales Managers Can Direct Maintenance

Because most of the emphasis of the district managers had been on sales volume, they had naturally not been especially concerned about using maintenance money well, even though the maintenance budget was used to maintain service stations. The maintenance budget had belonged to the regional director of maintenance, who had supervised all maintenance work. District managers simply tried to get as much of the regional budget as they could to fix up their stations.

In theory, of course, maintenance had been well controlled, because there had been a regional director of maintenance in charge of all maintenance. This regional control of maintenance had seemed to make sense because the maintenance experts certainly should have known more about maintenance than a district manager who had advanced through the marketing chain. The regional director of maintenance had not been close to small, local maintenance problems, however, nor to their marketing impact because the region had included several states. In addition, instead of using local contractors, he had used only a few selected firms whose crews traveled throughout the region. He felt that he could then be sure of their work. The practice had increased windshield time and travel expense, however, thereby increasing maintenance costs.

The regional general manager then changed the organization of maintenance. Maintenance crews, as well as maintenance contracting responsibility for each district, were assigned to the district manager, along with a maintenance budget for the district. This switch in maintenance responsibility could be effected because the new performance index now made district managers accountable for the total district effect on profit; it was advantageous to them to use the best possible judgment in spending the district maintenance money for the best overall profit achievement in the district.

It may seem strange that the inexpert district managers should be expected to supervise maintenance work better than the experts, but they did. Why? Not because the district managers knew more about maintenance, but because they were closer to the needs of the territories. In addition, they could make local contacts for simple maintenance much more easily than a home-office expert could, and local contract work was often cheaper than a traveling crew. The prime reason for the effectiveness of district managers in maintenance, however, was that they were accountable for both sides of the maintenance equation: maintenance costs and the marketing achievements to be obtained from the costs.

It is a common error to assume that experts will do a better job than local, accountable "inexpert" people. This is frequently not true. Local, accountable people have other factors riding on their side. In this case the district managers got the right work done with less red tape and at lower cost.

Reduce Terminal Costs

The analysis then turned to terminal costs. Previously, two staff engineers had been assigned to help all the terminals as staff terminal-operation experts. They had not supervised the terminals directly but were staff experts who had been expected to guide and assist terminals in meeting their various problems; both engineers had been available to all the terminals. Here, too, it had been assumed that a staff person was a good replacement for accountable line in keeping an operation running smoothly. Instead of each being accountable for the efficient operation of a group of terminals, they generally helped all of them and acted as troubleshooters when big problems occurred.

The organization plan was then changed, and each of the staff engineers was made a line superintendent in direct charge of half the terminals. Each engineer was made accountable for the total productivity and service to the districts of the terminals assigned to him and controlled their people and their budgets. Since the district managers were now measured by the performance index (which included some terminal costs), they were more willing to cooperate with the terminals in getting lower costs. It was to their advantage to get good service at a minimum cost from the terminals. Terminal expenses and losses of product were reduced substantially at the same time that service to the stations improved.

Make Planning Pay

Another management function that had affected long-range regional productivity was the central planning department of the region. It had been costly and its contribution to the region had been disappointing. The planning work had been carried out by various regional planning people carrying out different functions in the department. The difficulty was that the work of individual projects had been fractionated: New-business representatives had found the locations for the stations and tied up the real estate; the legal section had handled the legal problems involved in getting the property; economic analysis had estimated profit potential, including the marketing forecasts and projected costs; engineering had planned and controlled the construction of the buildings. These different but related sections of a building project had not been tied together well, so the planning and construction of stations had taken extra time (both elapsed and applied) and had cost more than expected. Again, the department had been relying on specialists for the parts, hoping the parts would blend. They did not always synchronize well.

To improve the planning cycle and expedite the location and building of stations, all the parts (site location, legal, engineering, etc.) were put together under project managers who controlled all the work involved in completing a specific project. It was their job to coordinate all the work to complete successful stations on time and within cost budgets. The time to get the projects on stream was reduced. In addition, the work was done more efficiently, so the planning staff could be reduced. Regional central staff people for maintenance and engineering were then made part of the planning department, because they tied into the effective building of stations.

There was one remaining planning problem, namely, long-range planning; it had been mixed with the short range, and it had tended to lag. When short-range activities are combined with long-range in any planning or technical operation, the long-range activities tend to get short shrift, especially in a dynamic business. They get shoved aside by the urgency of short-range problems. In this case the vice president of sales then separated the long-range activities from the short-range to get better focus on the long-range planning needs. The long range was then less affected by urgent short-range problems.

Make Records Serve the Field

The analysis then turned to the effect of the regional accounting system. It had been expensive and had seemed to take a great deal of time to process items. In order to prevent errors, accounting had followed a careful philosophy of check and double check; "repaired by," "checked by," "approved by" on all the forms had indicated the number of checks even on small items. It had been assumed that control was best achieved through multiple checks. Accounting had wanted to be sure that no mistakes would go through the system. The extra checking also had caused a slower response time by accounting.

Accountants often lean heavily toward a double-check system for control, not realizing that the best control comes from stimulating people in the best direction.

The accounting approach was changed, and the accounting responsibility was redefined as that of a general auditor of operations, not as a verifier of minutiae. In addition, the regional head of administration was made accountable for value the region received from his records against their cost. He was thereby encouraged to critically analyze the contribution of his procedures. Many of the double checks were then eliminated; the additional return received from the double checks was not worth the extra time and cost. The administrative staff was then reduced. The record work itself was done faster with better service in the field.

HOW WAS REGIONAL ROM IMPROVED?

What was the significant feature of this analysis of a region? The region had to be viewed as if it were an independent entity with its own marketing problems, even though it was part of a national marketing operation.

The key to success was service to the final consumer. The vice president of sales changed the overall marketing philosophy from selling to the dealer to merchandising through the dealer to the final consumer. This philosophy deemphasized the central program approach in order to concentrate on local consumer problems. The new direction led logically to an emphasis on making the dealer successful as the best way to maximize regional accomplishment.

Dealer success, in turn, required that dealers be trained more intensively in merchandising techniques. In order to do this, the sales supervisors and the sales representatives first had to be trained to pass on these techniques to the dealers.

Profits were further maximized by encouraging each sales representative to concentrate on local problems instead of routinely following standard central office programs; they would follow only the programs that they thought applied to their territories. To further permit attention to local problems, district managers were evaluated by a profit performance index and, at the same time, given broader control of costs, pricing, and maintenance of service stations. They then had the tools to improve dealer effectiveness and maximize the return from the district.

Regional staff was directed toward improving service to the customer. As an aid to the sales representatives, the central marketing staff would put its programs into appropriate training form so that field people could better capitalize on the ideas of skilled staff in working with the dealers. New-station development was tightened by the use of project managers accountable for getting new stations on stream.

Long-range planning was given more attention by separating it from short-range site planning of stations. Line terminal superintendents replaced staff terminal experts; both the service from terminals and the cost of their operation were improved.

The information system was also changed to help field people in carrying out the consumer-oriented approach.

What was the result of this analysis of a regional operation? In three years, profit contribution was up 35 percent. There was an appreciable reduction in regional staff. Later, when the same approach was used for other regions, home-office staff was cut in half at the same time that the value of the staff to the field was increased.

9 Managing for Profitable Growth

A successful company usually makes its mark initially with one product line. After a while, it wants to branch out and grow profitably. This growth usually means going into different product lines and often into different businesses.

A management analysis must be sensitive to the special management problems a firm meets when it grows and diversifies. The successful practices that had built the original product line usually prove inadequate for the new business; new practices must be instituted to make the new businesses successful and maintain high ROM.

This requirement for change affected a growing subsidiary of a large company. It made small- and medium-sized air conditioners. Since it was the most profitable subsidiary in the parent company, the firm was naturally willing to pour more money into this subsidiary to make it grow further. The problem the president of the subsidiary faced in this analysis was how to manage the expansion so that it would grow steadily and, at the same time, profitably. What changes in management philosophy and procedures were required to do this?

A COMMON MANAGEMENT
STYLE IS NEEDED

As the subsidiary had diversified, there were frequently losses in profit because of inadequate action on problems, especially on the new problems that had developed. Many times, the lack of adequate action had occurred because people had been operating on different management wavelengths; a variety of management philosophies had been applied by different people. It had been difficult to get smooth coordination between different managers.

Get All Managers on the
Same Wavelength

As the firm had grown in size and in diversity, the president had hired a number of new managers from outside the company to fill new jobs. It had been necessary to keep pace with the growth; it had been hard to develop enough people internally with all the talents and skills needed. However, the president of the subsidiary had believed in decentralization and had, therefore, felt that managers ought to be allowed to run their own shows. This philosophy had been interpreted as allowing each manager to follow his or her own management methods. After all, the president had reasoned, a manager ought to be allowed to manage.

This kind of reasoning is an easy trap to fall into when a firm grows. While it seems logical on the surface, it causes difficulty in getting managers to tie in smoothly with others in working toward company results. Each manager is following different management approaches, and they may not jibe with the approaches of others.

Managers had naturally tended to use the management philosophy and the procedures followed by their previous companies; they had assumed that this background had been the reason why they had been hired. As a consequence some managers had been operating by General Motors methods, some by US Steel methods, and some by General Electric methods; in short, different managers had been operating by different management approaches. In itself each method had probably been good, but because of the variety, communication (and, as a consequence, cooperation) between managers had been difficult. In addition, it had been hard to transfer people between jobs; it had taken too long to adjust to the new management mode used by the manager of the new department.

Many firms have not recognized the necessity for a common management style for smooth integration of the management team; it is the cement that binds the team together to produce maximum ROM. In contrast, I think of the comment made in a well-managed, large company with a well-developed and universally applied management philosophy. "You can always tell an ABC plant." In that company management people were effective very soon after they were transferred to new jobs. They did not have to adjust to new management approaches. A common management style is especially critical for a growth company in order for all the people to understand the thinking of their managers and those of other departments with which they deal.

To correct the confusion caused by the various management modes of operation, the president worked out and published a company management style, covering principles of delegation, accountability, authority, policies, staff, and so on. It described the mode of operation of the company management. All managers were trained on these principles through films and were strongly encouraged to follow the management style. New people were then worked into the firm more easily; they could better understand the basis for management action in their own departments and in those with which they had to work. People coming from firms with different management modes of operation could more easily be assimilated. Necessary working relationships were improved; all management people were communicating on the same management wavelength. They could devote their time to accomplishing results rather than to trying to understand strange management modes of operation in order to relate to others.

Still Keep the Focus on Results

The practice of allowing each manager to operate by his or her own management style had led subtly to a heavier concentration on activities rather than on results; each manager emphasized a particular way of thinking (which seemed to lead to a particular way of managing) and backed it strongly. The evaluation of managers had further encouraged this approach because it had been heavily based on judgment factors—the way managing was done—also stressing activity. As a consequence, although the firm had an MBO system, in effect it had frequently focused on activities. This activity emphasis in appraisal can easily occur in any company but is more understandable in a company facing rapidly changing management problems because of growth; it then seems especially difficult to set up results objectives for various managers because the conditions they are facing always seem to be changing. The dynamics of the situation seem overwhelming.

As a consequence of this activity emphasis, individual managers had not felt fully accountable for achieving results in their positions; the changing management conditions had seemed to suggest more reliance on appraisals that focused on what seemed to be appropriate activities. Deviations from results had been acceptable if they were explained by acceptable action; "acceptable" usually meant appropriate to the problem, whether or not the deviations led to the results desired. In order to justify action later, therefore, managers had developed defensive files explaining their actions and the reasons for them. In addition, they had frequently referred problems to groups to solve. Through the process, accountability had been weakened.

The concentration on activities had been further encouraged by the tendency to fragment functions, to develop more and more specialists. The tendency had developed in this way. With the rapid growth of the company, productivity had dropped because many additional new problems had developed. Since all the managers had seemed busy already, the president had felt that hiring a number of specialists to fit the specific new problems that had occurred was the natural solution. It had seemed logical to strike at the many facets of new and different problems that were arising by breaking them down into their small, specialized parts for solution; the summation of these specialized solutions should have provided the overall solution. However, it had taken a great deal of management time to coordinate these specialties —to get the new specialists to work together toward overall corporate results. In addition, the process of coordinating these specialized solutions had tended to further centralize decision making. As a consequence, local people had not been able to react quickly to meet the changing conditions that they had to face— a critical problem during periods of rapid growth.

Further, in order to maximize the return from specialized knowledge, it had seemed sensible to have the specialists report to managers who in turn were specialists in the field, not to the line people that they served; in other words, it had been assumed that it took a specialist to supervise a specialist effectively. The specialists could then develop more rapidly in their specialties and, therefore, make a greater contribution to the firm. But the approach had removed specialists from line problems that they should have helped to solve; they had not identified themselves with these problems. Secure in the cocoon of their specialties, they had not developed a sense of urgency to solve line problems promptly—a critical need in a rapidly growing and changing business. They had emphasized their own specialized sections of work irrespective of their impact on overall line problems and had not been inclined to compromise their specialized solutions for the overall line results.

In addition, the emphasis on specialists had made it hard to develop broad managers—another critical factor in a growing company where additional managers are constantly required. Managers develop broad management perspective to make balanced decisions through accountability in a variety of jobs; when specialists are only promoted or transferred to jobs in their own specialties, they tend to look at all management problems from their narrow, specialized point of view. They have difficulty giving suitable weight to other disciplines. In order to meet the growing need for more generalized managers, the president had, therefore, had to go outside the company and hire broad, experienced managers as openings occurred. But as we indicated earlier, these people had management approaches that were different from those existing in the company; integrating their work into the company had been difficult. At the same time the specialists within the company who had been passed over had been unhappy over their reduced opportunity for promotion.

Beyond this, however, central staff had not been accountable for the line results that they had affected, especially for results in new line operations that had been added. For example, purchasing, materials control, and manufacturing services all had looked at the new Bogenville plant 1000 miles away as "They," almost as if it were a different company. Their prime attention had been focused on the highly visible, large plant near the home office. This plant, the oldest, had produced the regular products for a long time. There had been a consequent tendency to give "them" (Bogenville) poor service on their problems. The home-plant managers had received most of the staff attention. First, they had been close geographically; second, their problems had been familiar.

How was this condition changed? Wherever possible, the president combined specialties so that one person handled a broader aspect of a result. Fewer got into the act; there was less need to discuss a problem with another specialist and seek a compromise solution between the specialists involved. For example, design and production engineering were combined so that the same person would do both. There had been conflict between the two before. In addition, the president insisted that management objectives for staff people be based on meaningful company results in spite of the changing company problems caused by growth. They were then more effectively geared to help the line as the company changed. Since these results were usually operating line results throughout the company, specialists became concerned about the urgency of meeting line problems no matter where they occurred. This sense of urgency is especially critical in a rapidly changing operation.

Even though much of the emphasis in all functions had been on activity, in some cases results had been stressed; in those cases, however, the emphasis had been primarily on efficiency, not necessarily on balanced results. In a growth operation, especially, other results are often more important to expand the company in the future—because of timing requirements, change of procedure, need for sensitivity to new customer requirements, etc. To get managers over to balanced emphasis, all of them were trained in job purpose with growth in mind—teaching them how to analyze those results that they should be working toward in their jobs to tie in with growth expectation. The job-purpose analysis was changed in tune with the changes occurring in the company. Objectives were then set up based on these balanced results. Setting these objectives required a constant compromising between several desirable results, sometimes downplaying worthwhile current results in deference to those needed for future growth.

To make the results setup work well, staff, too, had to be held accountable for balanced line results, even when they were working on projects for the future; they had to balance reduced current achievement against future value. Both staff and line were made accountable for current and future line results, however, so that the company would grow soundly. It is a mistake to assume that only staff should be concerned about the future.

Finally, the president had to change the philosophy behind the recognition systems (pay and appraisals) so that they encouraged the new directions and gave impetus to them. These systems were changed to reward for balanced results leading to profitable growth. The rewards then encouraged work toward corporate goals.

Decentralize to Develop Managers for Growth

When the firm had been small and the product line had been simple, centralization had probably been all right. Everyone at the top had been familiar with current local problems. Communications had been good; people had talked to each other just about every day. Centralization had become an escape route upward, however, as the company had grown larger and more diversified; people had simply passed their problems upward. In order to get adequate information on what was occurring at lower levels in the company, higher managers had often bypassed intermediate managers and contacted people below; this action had further aggravated the supervisory relationships below. The higher managers had gravitated into the position of taking over responsibility for detecting weakness below and correcting it, though the higher management had not been completely familiar with the situation below. The whole process had weakened the sense of responsibility below, reducing total ROM.

As a natural consequence of the centralization of decision making, management development had not been viewed as an integral part of every manager's job; managers themselves had not been further developed because of the upward flow of decision making to the top. Centralization had, therefore, affected management development, a critical need for the sound growth of the company in order to provide managers to fill the new positions that were constantly developing. In addition, transfers between functions and between product divisions (a prime way to broaden managers) had been infrequent. Transfers between line and staff had also been infrequent, so managers had not fully learned the essence of staff-line relationships. As a consequence managers had become divisionally or functionally inbred and had not developed the broad perspective needed to meet new problems easily.

The results accountability commented on above was very helpful in decentralizing decision making and in developing managers; it encouraged them to take action in their responsibilities by making them accountable for accomplishment. They were then expected to take the necessary action. In addition, the president established the rule of completed work as a standard mode of operating; it was important in order to change direction, so a person who had been delegated the responsibility for a result was made accountable for that result, no matter who helped and no matter who was told about the problem. A manager could not duck accountability for solving a problem just because someone above entered into the picture; it no longer did a manager any good to flow problems upward. The fact that a problem was new made no difference; after all, in a growing company many problems are new. Managers were expected to constantly solve new problems. At first, this rule seems unfair in a growing company, but it is essential if managers are to grow to assume broader responsibility, a critical requirement of a growing company.

The president also set up a program to encourage cross transfers of managers between divisions and between functions; company management people could then be more broadly developed in-house. As a consequence, more of the new positions required by growth could then be filled adequately from inside the company, a more efficient way to increase ROM and a morale builder with employees.

BUILD NEW BUSINESSES

While the changes that were installed now gave a good basis for the sound growth of the business, a number of additional growth problems still remained. They revolved around the development of new businesses, which were to be the basis for future growth. The analysis had to take a different turn.

Broaden Procedures to Fit Growth

While the president had been able to maintain profit on the old product lines that had built the business, he had found it especially hard to get the increases in sales and profit on new businesses as they developed; the new international division and the new product lines that had been different from the standard lines were cases in point. There had been a natural bias in emphasis toward the original U.S. division and its standard products. After all, they had made up the business that everyone knew, and they had been successful over the years. It had seemed hard to argue with success. It had been assumed that the proven procedures effective for standard U.S. products would naturally apply in building other divisions and other products. The differences of new divisions and of new products had been minimized. In addition, the U.S. staff had found it easier to use the same methods that they had always been using in order to serve new divisions and new products; they had not had to go through the trouble of changing them. The trauma of change had been avoided. But the problems of the other divisions and of new products were often different from those of the regular U.S. business; different businesses usually require different approaches in order to solve their problems.

The problem of adjusting previously effective management procedures to meet the needs of new businesses is normal in any successful company that grows in size and complexity or becomes a conglomerate. It is hard for the successful management to change its proven approaches to fit the changing needs. It does not recognize that those same methods were proven in the first place by studying the peculiar problems of the old division—an analytical procedure now called for in the new divisions.

As a case in point, in this company manufacturing had been primarily geared to serve the basic products of the U.S. division, products that had been manufactured for some years. Manufacturing had, of course, perfected these procedures. It had, therefore, been naturally reluctant to make the changes in procedures that were needed if it was to help the international division serve the international customers.

Since the U.S. division had been a mature division, it had primarily pushed for efficiency. The international division had, therefore, found it hard to get the special service needed to acquire new customers, as well as that needed to satisfy the different requirements of its customers. Sales to some international customers might require changes in the products and also different shipping schedules. The problem had been aggravated by the fact that the manufacturing people had been held accountable on a cost-per-unit basis; this had seemed to be the best way to encourage ROM in manufacturing while producing the old products for the U.S. division. They had, therefore, been understandably resistant to any changes needed in their procedures to serve the international division better. For example, they had objected to increases in inventory or changes in schedules to fit the service needs of African sales. In addition, the cost system had resulted in charging the international division less than true costs for some of the service it required. The other new-product divisions had suffered similar difficulties in getting manufacturing service—all stemming from a lack of flexibility in manufacturing programs to fit their special needs.

Market to Fit Different Products

The analysis also had to reexamine marketing approaches. As part of the U.S. syndrome, there had been a tendency to market new products through the same channels as those used for the original product line of the U.S. division. In some cases these had been inappropriate; they had not related well to the customer requirements of the new products. For example, noncorrosive tubing, a new original-equipment-manufacturer (OEM) product, required an entirely different marketing approach from the one that was effective for standard U.S. products, which were essentially shelf items.

The marketing problem was aggravated because product managers had not fully guided each new product line for broad profitability. Product managers had been under the U.S. division management and had naturally followed procedures that had been set up to merchandise the original, standard U.S. product line. In many cases these procedures had not applied well to the other products or to the other divisions. In addition, although the product managers had had the responsibility to suggest prices, they had not been accountable for profit on their products. They had been most concerned with current sales. Beyond this, although all the product development work had supposedly been under the guidance of the product managers, they had not coordinated product development with marketing all the way through to maximize profit. Overall, they had not taken the responsibility for both short-range and long-range profit on their products and for the market planning, strategy, and follow-up tactics that would lead to it. They had not been fully tied to the field or to the manufacturing and engineering of products.

The president, therefore, expanded the responsibility of the product managers. They were made accountable for both long-range and short-range profit of their product lines. The president broadened their responsibility to include sound merchandising of their products, developing product lines, and liaison with all the interested groups in manufacturing and engineering to make the product profitable. Productivity of product managers then meant profit from their products; they coordinated all the work to make their products profitable.

Make Policy Flexible to Fit New Businesses

Besides the difficulty in relationships between departments, overall procedures had turned out to be overly restrictive when applied to international and new-product efforts. The U.S. procedures were used, but they lacked flexibility to fit the problems of these other areas; the U.S. procedures had been assumed to be an absolute reflection of the intent of the policy. They were for problems of standard U.S. products but not for the problems of new products or for other geographical areas. It had not seemed necessary to develop a policy stating broad corporate intent in manufacturing, marketing, new-product development, personnel, etc., with permission to let procedures vary to fit the division needs. In order to meet their problems, other divisions had needed different procedures from those that had been appropriate for the U.S. division.

The president then made the basic decision to establish corporate policy on a broad basis by clarifying its intent, but allowing differences of procedures in application in the different divisions. Policy that was U.S. policy only and applied only to the U.S. division was specified as such. International and other divisions might then have different operating policies and, therefore, different procedures to fit their needs, no matter what the function was that was involved, i.e., the U.S. division's approach for Detroit did not have to apply to Bogenville, serving another division.

Allocate Costs in Line with Growth

The profit of new divisions did not always come up to expectations. One of the reasons why new divisions had not developed profitably had been the way the cost system worked; costs had not been allocated according to the new requirements of service demanded by these new divisions. The international division and the new-product divisions often had different requirements from those of the standard U.S. division. In many cases the additional costs of these requirements had not found their way to these divisions because of the system of charging costs; the U.S. division was, therefore, unduly burdened with extra costs when helping the other divisions. Naturally, U.S. division executives had been disinclined to give the special service requested by the other divisions; it threw their budgets out of line because cost charges to the other divisions did not reflect the additional cost of the service given.

Cost accountants are often unconcerned about the management impact of apparently "trivial" changes in cost charges and allocations; different breakdowns in charges or allocations cause them more work. In a growing and changing business, however, it is absolutely essential to keep current realism in charges and allocations; otherwise, the very cost and budget systems can prevent the business from growing. The cost system may discourage necessary cooperation; in addition, both corporate and division executives cannot make sound cost decisions.

The president of this company then insisted that the cost system be changed so that both overhead and direct cost were more directly charged against the divisions that occasioned them; the change covered both direct charges and cost allocations. A division was then allowed to demand changes in procedures that fit the division, but it had to pay for them.

Divisionalize to Build Each Business

To further maximize the management drive in all areas of the business, the president decided to divisionalize as far as possible. He set divisions up, as much as possible, as profit entities. Each major product line was set up as a division, as was the international division. Each had the overall obligation to capitalize on its markets and to maximize profit and growth of the division. As part of divisionalization, each division was then allowed to make most of the decisions on all aspects of its business and was made accountable for their impact as far as possible. Each division was looked at as an independent business. In order to make the divisionalization effective, the president required that the cost system reflect the impacts of decisions made by each division so that divisions would be charged the true costs.

As part of the divisional philosophy, a strong effort was made to have all the services a division needed report to it. Divisions were given as much control as possible of their operations, with the right to even go outside the company for service if they thought it was advisable for the best profitability of the division. To some extent, internal services then had to compete with services available outside the company.

In line with divisionalization, product managers were placed in the individual divisions that they served. The international division, for example, was given its own product managers, responsible for individual product profitability internationally. Product engineering was also broken down in the same way, i.e., the international division was given its own product-engineering department to focus on suitable products for international customers. At the same time the organization of product engineering was changed so that engineering supervisors in the divisions supervised both electrical and mechanical engineers in the division. Previously, these disciplines had been separated by specialty under the assumption that the disciplines would then be stronger. The setup had required extra coordination of disciplines in the development of a product, however. It had also been hard to get firm engineering accountability for the overall design of a product or of a product change. The organization change reduced these problems.

Manufacturing for all divisions continued to be carried on in the same plants. On analysis, the president found that it was impractical for each division to have its own plants at this time. On an interim basis, therefore, all manufacturing was set up as a separate manufacturing division. It is a mistake to break up individual plants into sections just to force the sections into divisions; similar plant services, procedures, and union contracts must usually apply to all sections of a plant. However, along with broader manufacturing control, the central manufacturing division had to assume the obligation to serve all the business divisions according to the needs of each; different manufacturing procedures might therefore apply to the work for different divisions if they demanded any special service. The manufacturing division included purchasing, manufacturing control, manufacturing, and plant engineering. The business division managers would get manufacturing advice from manufacturing, but they would make the decisions as to what they required. They would be charged for whatever service they requested for their divisions, however. In essence, then, manufacturing was temporarily set up as a major service division for all the other divisions. It had the obligation to serve them according to their needs. As the business divisions grew, separate plants might be considered for each, reporting to the division manager of the business.

ORGANIZE TO DEVELOP
NEW PRODUCTS

The area of new-product development required additional analysis because company growth had often been retarded due to a delay in the launching of new products. While everyone had wanted new products generally, in practice the emphasis had been on improving the standard U.S. product line. In addition, current profit emphasis had made it difficult to give weight to new product work.

For Growth, Separate R&D from
Product Development

A major cause of new-product lag had occurred because the R&D on new products was looked at in the same way as the changing of old products to meet changing customer requirements. In essence there had been little distinction made between product engineering for the change of standard products and the more experimental R&D required for new products, whether for a new line or for a new product to augment the present line. As happens so frequently in this kind of situation, the urgent, current customer requirement on the standard line had tended to get the emphasis; the orders were on hand. The longer-range new-product development had gotten short shrift; the orders were in the future. This problem frequently occurs in medium-sized growing companies; the urgency of current customer problems overrides long-range development, and as a consequence, growth is retarded.

In a way, the new-product problem had been recognized in the company. In order to cope with it, the firm had tried to define R&D projects by the length of the project; longer projects were classified as R&D projects. But this classification had not worked well because some engineering projects on changes of current products could have taken just as long as true R&D projects; time on a project had not been a good gauge. Besides, there had always been pressure on current products no matter what the length of the project because there had been customers to satisfy.

The president then decided to take a different approach in order to give new emphasis to new products; most of the normal changes in the current product line were put under the engineering heads in the business divisions themselves. It was their job to satisfy current customers. A central R&D department was set up with the obligation of developing new product lines or of working out major changes in existing product lines. This department was, therefore, engaged almost entirely in longer-range projects. The measurement of its success was the increased profit realized in the future from the new products they developed.

Get New-Product Emphasis with a New-Product Manager

To make the new-product program work well, however, a close tie-in with the marketplace was needed. Customers had to buy the new products once they were launched. The president, therefore, set up the position of new-product manager. This person was to take the responsibility for guiding new products from a feasibility stage through to marketability, whether they were new product lines or major changes in existing products. The new-product manager was not required to make any assumptions as to manufacturing, marketing, or engineering techniques until they were proven to be sound for the new product. This open-management approach is critical for new products so that they are not strapped by methods of the original product line which do not apply. The function of the job was simply to maximize the profit potential of the new product using whatever methods were suitable.

To give added stimulus to new products, a project review committee was also set up, made up of key people from different functions: manufacturing, marketing, engineering, accounting. They would review new-product ideas received from any source, consider their potential for the company, and make recommendations to the new-product manager on whether or not they should be pursued. The new-product manager, in turn, would make recommendations on new products to the president. This committee was chaired by the new-product manager; it was, therefore, the new-product manager's responsibility to guide it to recommend worthwhile new-product projects.

The president retained the final authority for approving projects on new-product ideas recommended by the new-product manager; he made decisions on the allocation of funds after receiving and accepting these recommendations. He determined their overall fit into the business of the company. He also retained the authority to decide on project cancellations and major changes in new-product projects, if they were necessary.

After the product had been proven ready for commercialization, the new-product manager would make recommendations to the president on folding the new product into the company structure; only then would the decision be made as to whether it should be part of an existing division or whether it should be set up as a separate division. The president would then decide how to integrate the new product with the rest of the business.

Reduce Prototype Lag

Prototypes (working models) had tended to lag in production because manufacturing had been penalized when producing prototypes. This lag had, in turn, delayed the completion of product-engineering projects. Manufacturing people had been on cost objectives and had been given no special credit for the extra time that might be required to give prototypes the special handling they required (short runs, quick timing, special tolerances). All this time was then taken out of any charge against manufacturing cost; it was, therefore, no longer disadvantageous to manufacturing to do this work. Relieving manufacturing of the charges for these costs may appear to encourage extra costs. True, but the cost of prototypes is usually a minor factor compared to the value to the company of high quality and quick timing in getting out prototypes.

GROWTH MEANS CHANGE TO MAINTAIN ROM

This analysis highlighted the coordination that was necessary between functions and between people in order to accommodate to growth and maintain ROM. Growth would mean change in operation, substantial change. The whole management process was changed to encourage growth, smoothly and profitably.

The management style was broadened and formalized to adjust to change and to quickly assimilate the many new people that were required for growth. The new management style geared all management people to focus more clearly on results, even in a changing company. It pulled away from a concentration on activities and made management people more sensitive to the changing requirements for balanced results as the business grew. In order for the growing central staff to make contributions to growth, they, too, were made accountable for the changing line results that they affected.

The tendency to fragment functions was checked, and functions were combined in order to react quickly to the changing requirements in the growing company. Otherwise, the firm would have been swamped in an ever-increasing flood of competing specialists.

Decentralization was encouraged. The natural tendency to centralize decision making in order to force new directions was curbed, and decisions were decentralized and redecentralized— a never-ending process in a growing operation if it is to avoid stagnation.

Management development was emphasized; it was facilitated by accountability for results and by cross-divisional as well as cross-functional transfers to broaden the perspective of managers. The firm could then grow more healthily from within.

Decentralization led naturally to divisionalization in order to capitalize on all the markets. In order to maximize the growth of each business, each division was given control of all its needed services so that it could get prompt action on its problems. Since the firm had not grown far enough to put manufacturing into the business divisions, all the manufacturing was combined into a manufacturing division as a service division with the obligation to provide the manufacturing service that the other divisions needed.

Policies were broadened to further build new businesses. Policies now allowed for maximum variations in procedure within corporate intent to meet the exigencies of the individual divisions. The practice of applying successful procedures of the U.S. standard product line to other product lines was eliminated. In line with the broadening of policy, the positions of product managers were broadened to build profitability on all products and to tie manufacturing, marketing, and product development together for each product. Cost allocations were also reviewed, changed, and then reapplied in light of the changing management needs of each of the new divisions.

New products were given additional impetus by separating the R&D of new products from engineering on current products. A new-product manager took on new products, as they were developed, to make them commercially successful and keep them from dying in the mire of old and inappropriate methods. New products were given additional stimulation (and control) through a project review committee whose objective was to find and recommend profitable new-product projects. Finally, the prototype work was freed from the restrictions of normal manufacturing procedure in order to improve quality and timing on prototypes.

All the changes were needed to maintain high ROM as the firm grew.

10 Managing Information for Higher ROM

Information can be the right arm of any manager, the aid and stimulus necessary to reach maximum accomplishment. It can be a strong, positive influence on productivity. The difficulty is that information is frequently looked at primarily as a control instead of as a stimulus to ROM. In addition, data often seem to have surface validity: "The facts speak for themselves." On analysis, they almost never do; they require interpretation along with other information in order to fit the problems of the moment. It is not the information itself that is critical but the way it is interpreted, presented, and then used by managers. It is a positive influence only when it is used correctly. If it is used well, it can assist any manager in the organization in getting greater accomplishment. To be of assistance, however, information should primarily be used to help correct problems, not to set the blame.

One of the difficulties with information on the

achievement of a worthwhile result is that there is always another result affected which may not be reported on; the information reported on one result may create extra emphasis on that result just because it is reported. The result that is not reported on is deemphasized, causing imbalance. Other items affected must be analyzed and data on all results presented in perspective so that the best possible decisions are made on the problem. Otherwise, the information reported turns out to be a narrow control on only one aspect of the operation, with a negative effect on the total operation. It puts pressure on only some of the results that should be achieved.

Computers can accentuate the problem. They can greatly increase the value obtained from information, but they can just as easily mislead. Printouts seem to be so complete; all the information seems to be there. Therefore, there is a strong tendency to assume the decision is almost automatic, that no further analysis is necessary. This is an illusion. Decisions still must be made creatively in light of all the factors affecting a problem; compromises must be made between various forces that affect a management decision. Reports only give data on certain parts of the problem that are needed to arrive at a compromise. Putting reports into perspective must be considered part of any management analysis.

PUT COSTS INTO PERSPECTIVE

The prime problem in many information systems is that costs tend to be overemphasized. Current breakdowns in cost data always seem to be available; they are easy to accumulate. Current data on positive accomplishments or lack of accomplishments is frequently not as complete; as a consequence a bias develops toward cost emphasis.

Broad Cost Cuts Can Be Expensive

A natural increase in cost emphasis occurs when a company suffers reverses and experiences a decline in profitability. At that time it is tempting to do blanket cost cutting across the company.

However, although it is known that costs in the company are high because of reduced volume, all the managers seem to have a good justification (at least in their minds) for not cutting their budgets. No manager relishes cutting. Rather than forcing a deeper analysis, an executive, in desperation, then declares uniform cuts for all. Unexpected losses usually result from such blanket cuts.

For example, one large company suffered a decline in profit. It looked at inventory compared to sales, and felt that it should be able to free capital by cutting inventories 25 percent and still give reasonable service. The word went out to all division managers to cut inventory accordingly. The divisions selling shelf items could meet the objective without sales losses. However, one large division sold systems for the contracting trade. In this work you may deliver ninety-nine parts of the system promptly, but if you are late on one item, the whole project may be held up and the contractor may have to pay penalties. In other words, deliveries must be 100 percent on time according to promise dates. But the explanation of this characteristic of the business was not reported to the chief executive along with the inventory reports. The vice president of the division was unable to convince the president that the division should not be held to the general inventory cut. The loss in profit caused by cutting inventory in this division was greater than the profit realized from all the combined inventory gains made in the entire company. The firm lost its reputation as a dependable supplier.

Cost Information Alone Does Not Control Costs

Because cost information is often very complete, it is easy for an executive to be deluded and to assume that cost reductions indicated in a report *will* be cost reductions in fact. But wishful thinking on a report is not real life. Cost information by itself does not control costs; people control costs. It is true, however, that the information may be very effective in helping people locate possibilities of cost reduction.

There was an interesting twist on cost control in a paper plant. Rather complete records were kept on costs down to every foreman's crew; in the comptroller's opinion, the plant had a complete control of costs. He had not analyzed the cause of costs deeply enough, however. I was talking to one of the foremen and asked him whether he was overstaffed. He said he was, but this is what he was up against: The company had a rule that every order had to be shipped out during the week in which it was received. The rule made sense because of the nature of the business of their customers. However, if an order came in on Thursday and overtime was required to get it out because the week's schedule was filled, the foreman had to get the approval of both the superintendent and the plant manager individually—a good control, presumably. This foreman said that he had always been able to get the approval—after a great deal of discussion—but he had always looked bad.

"So," the foreman told me, "I get myself ahead on Monday, Tuesday, and Wednesday. Then if a rush order comes in on Thursday, I tell them, 'I don't know, you know it's Thursday. I'll do my best.' They say, 'Well, do your best, will you?' "

"I do," he said. "I always ship my orders out on time. I don't have any overtime, and I'm a hero in the front office. What would you do?" I told him I'd probably do the same thing. It was the only way he could maintain his position under these circumstances.

The plant manager then put the foreman on an accountability basis of cost per unit of output. All overtime controls were taken off. Within six months he cut his staff by five people.

A common error is to have experimental parts run in the regular production plant but not to give the plant credit for the fact that the parts are experimental, that extra time and attention are required compared to normal production. Such a setup indicates that the management analysis has not gone deep enough. Production people are then simply given credit for the parts produced as if they were production parts. Since experimental work requires a great deal more time for special setup and running, the plant people lose credit because of the extra time required every time they run an experimental part. Their inclination is to defer the part to a convenient time and, when they do run it, to do so as quickly as possible without considering extra quality requirements. The result may be poor timing for product development, less-than-needed quality of the experimental part, or both. It is far better to take the cost of this part out of their cost budget entirely and give them, in a sense, a free ride. It is critical that experimental work be done right and that it fit the timing of the project.

Budgets May Increase Costs

Budgets are a prime illustration of an overemphasis on cost. Action for the future is discouraged because the current budget will be negatively affected.

In one well-managed company the maintenance management was paid a bonus based on an expected 4 percent reduction per year in maintenance costs. Maintenance had met this requirement every year for several years—evidently it had done a superior job. In a deeper analysis of operations the firm discovered that machines which should have lasted ten years were only lasting eight and machines which should have lasted eight were only lasting six. In other words, the firm was losing in the life of the machines because of the "successful" bonus plan. When a machine was worn out, it was not hard to get engineering to approve an AFE for a replacement. The vice president of manufacturing had to work the longevity of the machines into the record system and bonus plan in order to get balanced emphasis.

In a large sales force, the budget put pressure on the number of salespeople in the field—a sort of district head count. The firm came out with a timely, new electrical product which did not sell. Why? District managers would not put on the additional promotional people that were necessary to get sales of the new electrical product on the way; they wanted to be within their budget of sales cost compared to current volume of sales. The vice president of sales had to increase their budget with specific extra allowances for electrical salespeople and then set reasonable current objectives for electrical sales to get the new product going.

Don't Sacrifice the Long Range

Many people have bemoaned the tendency of organizations to sacrifice long-range results for short-range results. Many accounting practices actually have built-in encouragement for this myopia. They exert constant pressure toward short-range results.

For example, one retailing company required store managers to absorb the cost of management studies in their current budget. Under accounting practice these were classified as current expense, not capital expense; the practice probably had its origin in government tax rules. The purpose of these studies, however, was to get a management setup that would be effective in the years following; it would be unusual if a store would get a major return in the same year in which the study was run. Because of the accounting practice, one store manager did not contract for a management study, even though it was clearly needed. The manager did not feel that the store should incur additional expense at the same time that all the staff people were being asked to cut their budgets to the bone. Projects for the future require future accountability and, therefore, measurements in the future, or else they are mired by short-term problems.

Strangely enough, emphasis on profit or on return on investment is often antagonistic to long-range success even though these factors appear to fit long-range goals of profit. The measurements are usually for the current year. The executive being measured is therefore discouraged from passing up current profit by spending to improve future profit; future profit does not appear in current-profit tabulations. Frequently, executive incentive plans fortify this emphasis on the short range because the payoff is based on the results of the current year. I have seen very few executive pay plans that adequately balance current results against future results. And yet chief executives will agree that a prime responsibility of a division manager, for example, is to make decisions today that will ensure a stronger division five years from now.

Intracompany Cost Transfers Can Decrease Profit

Productivity is affected in many companies because of the way interdepartmental accounting transfers of costs are handled. If one department or division does some work for another, what is the basis on which the other department or division is charged? Very often, accounting practice on these charges is antagonistic to profit and to management cooperation.

In one company the president held plant managers accountable by profit on the output from their respective plants. (This type of accountability is questionable to begin with.) The cost of any work done at one plant for another was transferred to the second plant at cost, however. The accountants justified the practice with the comment. "It's easier. Besides, it's all company money anyway." To a plant manager, however, this system made it detrimental to do something for another plant; a plant manager got credit at cost on his or her budget for such work but was held for profit on the total output. The more work a manager's plant did to help another plant, the poorer the results appeared. Consequently, plant managers would try to do as little as possible on such work and would put it off as long as possible. At the same time, a "receiving" plant got a "gravy ride"—credit for the profit on goods-in-process received at cost. To correct the problem, the president had to change the accounting to give plant managers credit for all transfers to other plants at market price, which included normal profit.

In some companies transfers between divisions are made at a cost plus normal profit (really a cost-plus arrangement), which might be higher than the market price. The first division is, therefore, credited with a profit which may not be justified, and a burden is imposed on the second division. The total profit picture of both divisions is unrealistic, leading to poor executive decisions and lower ROM.

Don't Rely on the Indirect-to-Direct Ratio

A popular device of many controllers for controlling costs is the indirect-to-direct cost ratio; it compares the costs of all indirect people, staff and supervision, with the direct costs of first-level production workers. It is usually applied to plants, but at times it is used for sales departments too. Accountants assume that it is a good measurement of management efficiency.

The indirect-to-direct emphasis is based on the logical proposition that only the first-level direct workers affect production. It assumes that the lower the proportion of indirect people, the more efficient the operation. Obviously, in grossly overstaffed operations or those that misuse staff, this could be true. Otherwise, it is patently false.

Take a highly technical and growing industry like electronics. Innovation, a necessity for very survival, depends on large numbers of engineers pushing the state of the art for technical advantage in the future. In addition, products and processes are constantly changing, requiring additional staff and supervisory time to develop processes and train people in them. Productivity depends on the wise use of extra staff and supervisory people. The survivors in the industry will probably have a high proportion of indirect people. Granted, the firm must use these indirect people wisely.

Even in a mature business, whether it is manufacturing, merchandising, or financial, added productivity usually comes from the intelligent use of staff people, whether they are engineers, product managers, or computer specialists. The sharpest executives will use staff effectively to run the business, but they may have a high ratio of indirect-to-direct workers. On the bottom line, they have the best ROM.

MAKE INFORMATION INCREASE ROM

There is a tendency to assume that information managers only have a responsibility to provide information to others and that they cannot personally contribute to accomplishment. After all, the line makes the decisions. This view does not capitalize on the positive potential of information people. They can be and should be looked upon as positive contributors to the success of the operation.

A Credit Department Can Increase Sales

Imbalance often occurs in a credit department because of the tendency to overemphasize credit losses, since that information (like cost information) is readily available. A minimum of data is collected on lost sales caused by tightened credit or on unrealized sales potential. These lost sales are difficult to measure, but as every sales department knows, they are there. The purpose of credit should be to get more sales, not to chase them away; it should be aimed at building customers—customers who pay their bills. Credit losses should always be recorded in some way against sales lost because of tight credit restrictions. Credit managers will then be encouraged to look at credit from a creative sales point of view and to minimize excessive credit risks.

A chemical company suffered a substantial decline in sales during a recession. Many customers became poorer credit risks. The credit manager applied traditional credit approaches and tightened up on credit. She also shortened the aging permitted on accounts at the time when customers were trying to use supplier inventories by delaying payments on bills. The effect was a further dampening of sales.

The credit manager decided to creatively use credit policy to help sales. She got the approval of the general manager to liberalize credit selectively, with the aid of the vice president of sales. The vice president of sales was inclined to help because his bonus depended on profit. The two agreed to accept more delinquencies among those vibrant accounts that had potential for the future. They built more sales, customer good will, and, in the business upturn later on, they increased their market share.

I remember an innovative credit manager of a small shoe company who was responsible for much of the company's profit. The company's market position made it difficult to get any but third-class credit accounts, the kind that many credit managers turn down. This credit manager disregarded most standard credit-ratio data and account financial histories. He creatively approached these accounts like a financial consultant by helping them become solvent. As a result, the company developed good business from these accounts and got paid. The firm was more profitable than most of the big shoe companies in the industry.

Make Accounting Charges Increase Management Return

A popular theory in accounting is the controllable expense theory, which simply says that you charge the expense against the manager who does the work. This is logical. A manager who is charged with the cost will probably try to do the work as efficiently as possible; if you are charged with a cost, it is to your advantage to keep it at a minimum. However, a person who might minimize the need for the expenditure in the first place is often not charged for it. The first question in minimizing costs is: *Can the cost be prevented?*

For example, in one company a central purchasing department got a "good buy" on parts from a supplier in Australia. When the parts arrived, they were nonstandard and could not be used as they were. It took a great deal of inspection and rework time at the receiving plant to make the parts usable. Under the controllable expense theory in effect, all of this cost was charged against the budget of the plant manager of the receiving plant where all the inspecting and reworking was done. None of the cost was charged against the purchasing department because it did not do the inspecting or reworking. Purchasing assumed that it had made a good buy because it got the parts cheaper, and this fact appeared in its records. However, the costs of rework, inspection, and delays were greater than the savings made on purchasing the part. Purchasing should also have been charged for these so that it would consider in-plant costs as well as up-front prices when buying.

Under the controllable expense theory, warehousing costs for finished goods are charged against manufacturing in some companies because manufacturing operates the warehouses. However, many decisions that affect warehousing costs (inventory levels, service, etc.) are often made by the sales department. If the total cost of finished-goods warehousing is charged to the sales cost of the sales department, sales will do more creative work to keep inventory to a minimum, to work off obsolete inventory, and to minimize special order-handling demands of customers.

Similarly, purchasing, maintenance, engineering, and sales all have impacts on downtime in various companies. If the cost of downtime in a plant is only charged against the plant and not against the other departments that may affect it, these other departments are not encouraged to do what they can to minimize it. The downtime must be broken down into those parts that are affected by each of these other groups, and they, too, should be charged for the downtime costs accordingly. Double accounting is necessary; the production people should still be charged for downtime costs. The charges will then encourage the service departments to work with line production management to cut down on downtime.

The record system can discourage efficiency in any in-house service. For example, if an in-house machine shop does work for various engineering departments, all engineers are ordinarily encouraged by higher management to use it. This is a "captive" machine shop, and the engineering projects are usually routinely charged for the work at cost. The arrangement seems logical, but it does not encourage efficiency in the machine shop. One way to sharpen the machine shop up is to make it compete. For instance, allow engineers to go outside the company for the machining they need on their prototypes. Another way is to force the machine shop to charge competitive prices and use these charges instead of its costs. The obvious difficulty is the determination of competitive prices.

In determining the cost of developing a new product, there is a tendency to assume that development costs of the new product only carry up to the point where the designs are released to production. Accounting then cuts off all charges against the development project and assigns them to production. In many cases installation costs in the plant may be as great as or greater than the original development costs and could be reduced by the design engineers. All these installation and redesign costs should be considered part of the cost of developing the new product and should be charged against the project. If they are, engineers will more carefully weigh production and redesign problems when determining their designs. The director of an electronics laboratory obtained a drop of 50 percent in the cost of getting new products into production by this change in accounting philosophy.

Cost Allocations Can Retard Action

Cost allocations are usually made for accounting's convenience in line with the accounting practice in the company, but they affect ROM at all levels. The first rule of allocation should, therefore, be that, wherever possible, costs should be charged against a department or section instead of being allocated; in other words, allocation should be a last resort and only used if direct charges are not feasible. And the feasibility decision should not be affected unduly by any additional accounting costs that might be involved; it may take a little more clerical time or a little more computer programming, but it is almost always worthwhile in terms of the stimulation of management. Allocations rarely stimulate managers to action, but direct charges often do.

For example, one machining plant had a high accident rate. It had tried making foremen accountable for their own accident frequency rate, but this had not seemed to have any effect. In line with central accounting's decision, the total cost of all accidents in the plant was allocated to the budgets of the plant departments on a per-direct-employee-hour basis. A small accident each month for five months did not disturb a foreman. If a severe accident occurred in a month, the foreman's reaction was, "The employee was just careless."

The system of charges for accidents was then changed. First, foremen were held accountable for cost per unit of output of their crews. The cost of any injury that amounted to more than $100 was charged directly against their cost budgets. A bad accident might throw off a foreman's costs for several months. Within six months accidents were cut about 40 percent. It may seem strange to get action on safety by cost accountability but in this plant that turned out to be the best method.

In a small company sales had increased nicely but profit had declined. There were three product lines and, for ease in accounting, order-handling and product-engineering costs were allocated to each product line based on dollars of sales. One product line required very little product engineering; it was made up of standard shelf products. In addition, it was sold in large orders which meant that order-handling costs were very low. Another product line was just the opposite; it was a job shop business, and sales volume was made up from many small orders. Each order required special engineering, and orders were small; therefore, product-engineering and order-handling costs were high per dollar of sales. The effect of this allocation was to place the costs and, therefore, the prices of one division too high; they were not competitive, so volume declined unnecessarily. In the other division listed costs and prices were too low; while sales increased substantially in this division, profits declined because the products were underpriced. Their CPA had recommended the allocation system for accounting efficiency.

In many firms various central staff and service costs are frequently allocated on an overall basis such as per dollar of payroll. If possible, staff costs should be charged where the service is used. Staff people are usually more effectively applied under these circumstances.

Base Decisions on Real Costs

In one large company selling electrical equipment, the accounting department of a division was constantly putting pressure on the sales department to push small orders because the profit margins were 40 percent. On large orders they were 20 percent because customers were given lower prices based on volume. Obviously, the accountants reasoned, there was a large profit potential in small orders. The trouble with their reasoning was that they, themselves, allocated sales expense on a sales-dollar basis. A salesperson might have to make several calls on a customer to get a small order (sometimes the same number as on a large order). Because the orders were small, order-handling costs were much higher per sales dollar on small orders. In addition, small buyers were less sophisticated in the technical aspects of the equipment; they required more free service work in the warranty period to make the equipment operate. Since all three of these expenses (cost of calls, order-handling costs, and warranty-service costs) were assigned on a sales-dollar basis, the apparent profit on small orders was an illusion. The accountants were misdirecting the sales department.

The sales costs of a china company were high because the firm sold directly through retail stores; the sales department spent a great deal of selling and merchandising time with each store. The firm had an opportunity to sell a large order of a desk decoration directly to a gift house. The president insisted that this order should carry the same ratio of sales expense as the other orders, even though it was a large house account of a single product requiring little sales expense and no merchandising expense; that was the president's interpretation of cost accounting. The firm, therefore, lost what would have been a very profitable order—little sales expense; the inflated price was not competitive. In addition, the order could have been run in a month when the plant had few orders, so it could have carried overhead.

In a short-run stamping business, the company accounting system did not differentiate between orders that repeated and those that did not. The company insisted that the dies be paid for on the initial order, since there was no assurance of a repeat order; the accountants insisted that this was sound accounting. As a consequence the firm did not receive many repeat orders; its more perceptive competition bid lower on these and got the business. The competition anticipated profitable repeat orders; because these orders were repeated using the same dies, they were still very profitable even at lower prices.

Cost philosophies are often not in tune with sound management. In one company a warehouse handled two different products. One was of high value but it weighed little; the other was of low value but it was heavy and bulky. Warehouse costs were allocated by dollar value of the product. An industrial engineer could not justify a methods improvement because under company policy standard cost had to be used in computing the present cost of a method to be changed. The product studied was a low-value, heavy product. The time study of the new method showed no improvement compared to present standard cost. In practice the new method would have made a substantial saving compared to the actual cost of the method being used.

Make Computers Serve

The advent of the computer has been a boon to management. It can be a powerful force in management, but like every powerful force it must be used properly to contribute; otherwise it, too, can become a negative force developing pressure against accomplishment.

Commonly held views on the place of the information flow have themselves been obstacles to productivity. Initially, executives had not understood the computer and had distrusted it; they did not then capitalize on some of its benefits. This attitude turned, in many cases, to an almost slavish dependence on the computer and on computer specialists. The flow of information from the computer was so great and apparently so complete that they assumed answers should be self-evident from the numerous printouts. They are finding that this reliance on computer information is not justified—as some perceptive computer specialists had warned. The input of computer people, like that of all specialists, must be blended with the inputs of others in order to get sound management solutions to problems. Computer information must be used with sound judgment.

The computer is a wonderful tool for managers, but it is just that, a tool. Essentially, it is an extremely high-speed adding machine with a marvelous memory. When these attributes are properly used, a computer is helpful. But note that I said *helpful*. Usually, additional inputs of judgment are needed both in programming in the first place and in the interpretation of the data.

For example, computers do not ordinarily make sales. When computers of customers are directly hooked up with retailers or suppliers, they get close to doing that, however. Merchandising, advertising, and sales servicing may still be required as a minimum.

In plants, products are not produced entirely by computers. Even in so-called automated factories, changes in programming and in the maintenance of computing and production equipment still require personal inputs. In some services a computer can go far, but even then problems seem to occur repeatedly that require additional judgmental inputs to solve them.

Since many information systems initially started in accounting departments, they often have an accounting slant; they are based on a philosophy of fitting the needs of accounting statements. This tendency is frequently not helpful to management in running the operation; it may even be detrimental.

In order to get around these computer difficulties, an executive should establish several policies and setups on information. First of all, information systems should be viewed primarily as a general tool for all managers to increase their productivity. This approach means that the computer systems should be based on the needs of all managers, not just on those of accounting. The information people should, therefore, be measured first by the value of their output to other managers; the cost of information should be a secondary factor. In order to keep perspective, the cost of information should be directly charged against the users, who should have the right, in most cases, to decide what information they should receive.

Wherever possible, the information flow should be decentralized to the unit using it. With the advent of small, cheap computers, this decentralization is possible to a great degree. Operations people, not professional computer people, should be trained to program and to use these computers wherever possible. People who know the operation are more likely to use the computer as a valuable tool. Computer specialists frequently lack knowledge of the operation the information is to serve. Special consulting by a computer specialist can, however, be made available on a sticky problem.

Overall, the executive should organize the information work to fit the line needs; this is what is meant by information systems "being a tool" for managers. The line should not be organized to fit the computer, as some executives have been inclined to do. Line people become frustrated and lose a sense of accountability under that approach. The computer people, in turn, are not accountable for balanced line results.

INCREASE ROM BY NONUNIFORM REPORTS

Information departments often like to issue the same kinds of reports for jobs that are similar; it saves programming and computer costs. However, different problems and, therefore, different objectives might require different information to be of maximum help to managers. In addition, different times might require different information because conditions may have changed. The information system should be flexible to reflect these differences.

A commonplace example of problems caused by uniformity is the uniform reporting of inventory; the reporting is frequently the same for different operations. The accounting department of a department store insisted on highlighting inventory turnover for all departments. As a consequence, a high-grade men's department was forced out of business. This department had to carry a number of slower-moving, high-style items in order to give its high-grade trade a choice; the margins, however, amply took care of it. Customers paying these high prices expected a good selection. The usual evaluation of inventory turnover was inappropriate for this department, even though it was perfectly proper for the basement store.

The president of a supermarket took me for a tour of some of the stores of his competition. We noted many empty shelves. He pointed out that the managers of these stores were heroes back at the home office because the stores had high inventory turnover and that was what was emphasized in the reports. Customers were getting a limited choice and were, therefore, going to competition, but that was not shown on the reports. The stores were doing about 70 percent of what they should have. The extra 30 percent was where the profit was.

When a recession results in lower sales volume, it is apparent that a company quickly becomes overinventoried. A president is inclined to issue an order for a blanket 10 percent cut in inventory because of pressure from the controller based on inventory compared to sales. This blanket approach is usually ill-advised. Even in this period one division or product line may be increasing its volume. Starving it on inventory because the company is overinventoried prevents growth at the very time that the firm desperately needs additional sales.

Further, in one plant much of the inventory may be obsolete. If a plant manager must accede to a demand to cut inventory quickly in a down period, production becomes even more costly in terms of lost sales because of inadequate supplies of the right inventory. The other alternative is for the plant manager to get rid of the obsolete inventory immediately by junking it. If the disposition is done more gradually, however, the firm may realize 50 percent of the value instead of 10 percent.

Similar Jobs Are Not the Same

It is easy to classify jobs in the same category because of the same job title; all jobs with the same title are assumed to be similar. Therefore, the same reports should suffice for all. Many information managers make this mistake; their assumptions are not correct. Jobs with the same title may have different problems. Using the same reports for all does not, therefore, encourage higher ROM.

For example, one sales territory may be new and growing. Another may consist of long-standing customers. The representative of the first territory needs growth data by product and customers. The second representative may need territorial data by product plus indicators of both trouble spots and high-profit situations.

One plant superintendent needs data by order and by the machine on which the orders were produced because the department is working on job shop business. Another, making shelf items, needs cost data by runs on each product plus variations compared to previous similar runs. Both superintendents may be in the same plant.

One manager of a mature division may need profit and sales data by product compared to that of previous years. The manager of a new and growing division may need data on growth of sales by product, by customer, and by the part of the country where the product is sold; immediate profit is not the major concern.

Different Levels Need Different Reports

A constant but natural error in uniformity is giving top executives the same reports as those given to people down the line. The argument advanced is: "After all, executives want to be informed too." Besides, with modern computers it costs little to run extra copies of any report, and an executive may get something out of it. The management requirement is different at different levels, however. Executives need combined data in order to make broader decisions. People down the line need detail to help them make day-to-day decisions. If executives also get these details, they naturally ask detailed questions of people way down the line. Minor errors are highlighted. (Executive cathode ray tubes, or CRTs, pose this problem.) In effect, executives subtly begin to run the operation several levels down the line; in the process, they weaken intermediate supervision below them. The whole operation becomes less productive.

On the other hand, many information managers resist breaking down records by individual foreman responsibility on the erroneous theory that "foremen can't make good decisions." The rationale is usually the lack of education of the foremen. On the contrary, any data that foremen need regarding the operation of their crews should be given to them, especially in a job shop. A little more work may be required on the part of the information people, but it is almost always well repaid by the constructive line action that it stimulates. This lack of trust in foremen is an increasing problem in many companies—foremen cannot make a decision because "they're not college grads." The extensive experience of some foremen makes them better able than college graduates to solve grass-roots problems.

In addition, many firms have found that there is no correlation between education and ingenuity. Some foremen have more ingenuity than many technically trained people have. Innovation is the major reason why companies become outstanding; it gives them an edge. It should be encouraged at every level of the organization, including the foreman level.

A Seasonal Business Needs Different Reports

Some companies are in highly seasonal businesses. The uniform reports in effect do not take account of these seasonal variations. The management problems in one part of the year are different from those in another. For example, in the airline business empty seats are a critical sales problem. Sales in off periods are much more valuable than overbookings in high periods. The cost and achievement data must reflect these fluctuations and thoroughly analyze the different areas, types of routes, and variations in customer potential demands in different seasons; higher sales cost per seat may be justified in certain periods.

In some seasonal companies, like a swimming pool company, most sales might be made in a three-month period. The cost value in stretching out these sales should be clearly pointed out in the information system. The plant could operate more smoothly with less overtime and fewer temporary people if sales could be pushed earlier by special discounts, financing, etc. In addition, customers could be given better service. The canning business is another example of a business with a seasonal problem justifying special seasonal data. Much of the produce comes to the plants during a few weeks. The records must reflect the crisis-type activity that must take place at this time. Seasonal businesses offer a special opportunity to increase ROM through the intelligent use of analytical data.

CREDIT DOUBLE TO INCREASE ROM

In most companies results come from the work of several people. Unrealistically, however, under typical accounting systems only one account can be charged for a cost or given credit for an accomplishment. The approach is a reflection of traditional accounting theory aimed at developing dependable financial statements. It does make sense in accumulating data for financial statements, but it does not make sense if you want your record system to encourage management cooperation and high ROM. From that point of view, two people (or more) should often be charged for a single cost and also credited for an accomplishment. How do you then straighten out your accounts for financial statements? You may charge or credit a second person on a management account that may be used for management evaluation but may not appear as a regular account in the accounting books. In this way the information system can be used as a positive tool to encourage both people involved to work cooperatively toward the same results; it is then advantageous to both to do this. A more sophisticated system of "washout" accounts can also be used.

Staff, Too, Should Be Credited

The standard accounting philosophy of crediting only one account has, in effect, led to no accounting for most staff impacts. Following this philosophy, staff people cannot be given credit for their achievements because, in the final evaluation, all their achievements are really line achievements. The costs involved have also been looked at as line costs and charged against line accounts. This approach shows up as unsound, if you want to increase staff's ROM. Staff people, too, should be credited both with the achievement and with the cost of the results that they work on.

Long-Term Projects Require
Long-Term Information

Long-term projects pose a special problem for a system of single accounting charges. An example is the development of new products. The work on them is only valuable when they finally result in sales and make a profit, usually after two to ten years; however, the cost, profit, and sales of new products are affected later on by other departments besides product development. The manufacturing department manufactures the product later, and the sales department sells it. There should be a postaudit of product results after the product has been sold for a while that leads to the charging or crediting of the original product development group with what actually happens to cost, sales, and profit on the new product when it is sold.

An engineering department that designs a new machine for producing product can be viewed in much the same way. A postaudit ought to be standard for checking all the additional maintenance that is required, as well as special operating problems that are occurring with the new machine. The cost of these should be charged against the design cost of the machine, even though these costs still remain as manufacturing costs. It is an excellent way to make machine engineers consider the total effect of the machine on the plant.

Charge People to Get Cooperation

It is especially hard to get double charges for a line function when another line function depends on it for service. There is also a strong tendency to view business divisions as independent, even though one relies on another for product, engineering, or sales service. This view often leads to lower ROM.

For example, people in a U.S. division of a company, like a U.S. bank chain, may have to do quite a bit of work to help the international division. They may feed in local customers who have international business. No credit is given to U.S. branch managers for helping the international division, even though in doing so they may even have jeopardized their position with their own customers. They must share in the credit for the ensuing international business if they are to be encouraged to help the international division grow. Managementwise they are probably compared to the international division managers in profit contribution. If they get no credit for international business they affect, obviously, they will not be enthusiastic about passing on customers to the international division.

In job shops, like printing houses or original-equipment manufacturers, the sales department should also be charged with the extra cost (special scheduling, setup, or design) required to produce for a specific customer's requirements. A good way to make this approach work is through the establishment of a system of profit on sales accountability for salespeople; they then get credit only for the net profit on their orders. The salespeople are then much more sensitive about the extra cost of any special customer request and try to work out alternatives with the customer.

Plants may have producing departments that have a considerable effect on the productivity of other producing departments. Unless the cost of the effect of one department on another is also charged back against the first department that may have contributed to it, the first department may not take vigorous action to reduce it. It may take extra time and increase the first department's costs. The succeeding department should still be charged with the costs, however, or else it might try to dump too much cost onto the previous department. Many times, both departments may have affected the cost, but it is hard to determine the relative effect of each. Accounting has a long way to go to meet this problem of accounting for dependent functions and encouraging cooperation between them.

INFORMATION IS A VARIABLE MANAGEMENT TOOL

In any management analysis it should be assumed that creative development and use of information can substantially increase ROM. The computer increases this opportunity. Many accepted approaches on records must be changed, however, in order to capitalize on records.

Information should encourage balanced accomplishment. Costs should not be overemphasized; a record or a budget does not by itself control costs, but people do. The information systems should encourage them to do so. Allocations and transfer of costs to various budgets must be made with this thought in mind.

The analysis should consider all the results affected. For example, a credit department can increase sales as well as minimize credit losses. Budgets should encourage long-range development of all types as well as short-range results. Slick accounting devices like the indirect-to-direct ratio and ROI should be reexamined for their negative effects.

Reports should be flexible because problems vary from day to day even between jobs that seem the same. Standard reports almost always encourage a standard of lower ROM because management problems vary. Seasonal changes may require different reports. Different levels in the organization also need different reports to reflect the different levels of decision making within the organization.

Information should encourage cooperation. Because much of the productivity in modern enterprise depends on cooperation between people, the information system should be reexamined to make sure that it encourages cooperation. Charging or crediting *more* than one person for an item should be standard procedure. Double charging or crediting is especially critical in long-term projects and between functions and divisions that could help each other.

With the advent of low-cost, high-capacity computers, there is an exciting vista for the contribution from information systems. Old systems must be rethought through, however, so that the information is a positive management tool. Yes, information is still primarily a tool for management, albeit a sophisticated and valuable one.

CHAPTER 11

Merchandising for Profit

The overall purpose of a retailing establishment is to move merchandise to satisfied consumers. This is usually done by meeting the customer demands in service and cost. Of course customers have to *feel* satisfied that they are getting good service at a reasonable cost. All this must be done within the context of competition. Generally, retailers are extremely competitive in luring customers.

In order to have a satisfactory business, however, merchandising must be carried out in such a way as to leave a satisfactory profit for the owners. A constant problem is the balancing off of service and price to a customer against company cost. In doing this, it is the total cost of the product and of the service, including all corporate costs distributed among the products, that determines overall product costs. Service of any kind to a customer costs money. In effect, it adds to the cost of the product. An executive must always weigh the added value to customers of any additional costs they incur. All costs, not just direct store costs, must be looked at in this way.

A problem of balancing off aggressive merchandising against corporate costs was well illustrated in a medium-sized supermarket chain. It had grown rapidly, and it expected to grow more. The company was starting to have growing pains, however; costly problems, and in many cases lower net-profit margins, were occurring. New stores did not always measure up to the profit that was expected. In addition, volume was not always up to what was expected. Volume is an especially critical problem in retailing because inventory turnover is a major factor in profits. The president of this chain decided to conduct a careful analysis of the total operation to see whether ways could be found to smooth over these problems, increase ROM, and ease the way for future profitable growth.

MAKE THE INDIVIDUAL STORE THE MERCHANDISING FOCUS

In carrying out this analysis, it became clear that the individual store should be the major concern. That was where the customer contacts were; it would be the critical point where success and failure would be determined.

Develop Store Managers

As the president carefully examined the total operation from the standpoint of the stores, he uncovered an interesting phenomenon, the excessive influence of the home-office specialist. As the firm had grown, it had seemed logical to add specialists in the home office to cover each of the major departments of a store—produce, meat, dry groceries, and so forth. These specialists had been experts in operating their particular departments in the stores and had been made responsible for upgrading them. As a consequence, they had assumed considerable authority and were very active in hiring, discipline, wage and salary increases, transfers and promotions, and even in setting store objectives and holding the department managers in the stores accountable for accomplishment. The approach had seemed logical because they were the experts in their fields.

A prime job of the specialists had been inspection: to see that their departments had been running properly in the various stores and producing satisfactory results. It had seemed natural, therefore, for the specialist to take on the responsibility of training the store personnel in the specialty. Since this work took a great deal of time, the number of stores handled by each specialist had to be reduced and more specialists were added. It seemed the best way to organize.

Obviously, specialists had not been able to be at the stores all the time; in their absence department managers had been on their own. For example, in produce the department managers in the stores had to make their own displays to fit the produce they had available. They had not been able to rely on the central produce specialist to help them all the time. On the other hand, they had hesitated to go outside of what the produce specialist had told them to do. Department managers, therefore, had not assumed responsibility for their departments.

As a consequence of the specialist setup, the store managers had not fully supervised their stores. They had not felt that it was their job. Supervision had in effect been taken over by the specialist. The store manager had become almost staff to the specialist.

To compound the store management problem, all invoices over $50 had been checked by the vice president of operation and by the general merchandise manager before payment. Invoices over $150 had been approved by the president. As a consequence, many of these transactions, simple or routine though they may have been, had been slowed down.

As this part of the analysis progressed, it became clear to the president that the key to the success of a store was to broaden responsibilities of the store manager and the department managers in each store. Oddly enough, this approach turned out to be the best basis for capitalizing on the skill of the specialists in the first place. The president decided to broaden the authority of the store managers and give them full control of all the people in the store. The store manager was not to surrender this responsibility to staff people. The staff specialists, in turn, were set up to train the department managers, so that they could do a more effective job on their own. To make the transition work, the president instituted a training program for all store managers and department managers in how to train, so that they could assume this full responsibility.

Make the Store Manager Accountable for the Store

But the president found that the new system could not work well because of the past history of the firm. As frequently happens, the problem setups in the past had caused the creation of compensating setups to bolster up the system. Because of the staff control, store managers had not felt accountable for the overall achievement of their stores but only for some of the costs under their control. They had not felt that they had really been in charge; they had only been coordinators. Even their direct store payroll had been strongly influenced by the specialists. The store managers, therefore, always had a plausible reason for inadequate results; it had been very simple to provide an alibi. They had not been truly accountable for store results.

On digging deeper, the president found that the system of management objectives had further discouraged the store managers from feeling responsible for the total operation of their stores. In many cases the specialists had strongly influenced the setting of objectives; as a consequence, a store's objectives had frequently not been based on the conditions it faced. Too little attention had been given to differences in conditions between stores. Beyond this, objectives that had been achieved in one year had often been simply moved ahead to the next year and increased. This approach had been followed even when there had been a decline in the potential in a store's area or when a new store had opened up just across the street. In other words, the objectives had often been unreasonable. The unreasonableness had been increased further by the controller, who had pushed for high inventory turnover (sales volume of a store divided by the market value of the inventory of products for sale). Inventory turnover lent itself to the figures that he worked with; the data were available. Having had access to the president, the controller had been able to put pressure on the stores through the president to keep inventories down even though the result might have been fewer sales and less profit.

The president then decided to change the whole system of recognition for store managers; he based it on net profit and growth of the particular stores. Further, the objectives of each store manager reflected the conditions faced in each particular store. If conditions changed, the objectives were changed. Inventory cost was included in overall profit but not set up as an individual item by itself. It was then up to the store manager to balance off all the different parts of the operation to affect the maximum profit contribution from the store.

District Managers Build Store Managers

After changing from store managers who relied on specialists and who were not fully accountable to managers that supervised their own stores and simply used the specialists as aides, a gap appeared as the president examined the arrangement more deeply. Since the specialists were not actually supervising as they had before, the store managers were supposed to carry on in place of them. In many cases they did not know how to do this. The obvious person to train them would be their superior, the vice president of operations. The vice president, in turn, could not do this because he had too many stores reporting to him; he did not have the time. That was probably why he had set up the specialists in the first place: to relieve himself of this work.

The president then established three district managers of stores under the vice president of operations. Each of them supervised several stores. It was the district manager's job to increase the effectiveness of store managers and build them up to meet their new responsibility. Each district manager had a manageable span of operation so that all the store managers could be adequately covered. It was the job of the district managers to develop and stimulate the store managers to take over their broadened responsibility and supervise the department managers in the store.

FOCUS CENTRAL STAFF ON
STORE RESULTS

In light of the changes in the store manager's position, the president now turned the analysis to a reappraisal of the positions in central staff. It became clear that their basic focus should be on supporting store managers to develop profitable stores. The company's strength was still its relationships with customers, and these occurred in the store. To contribute to company success, therefore, every central staff person should help meet the overall objective of giving customer service at a profit.

Many of the central staff people had been evaluated primarily by the way that they carried out their own functions by themselves, without necessarily looking at the total balanced effect on each individual store. They had not been in complete tune with store operations. The president decided to change this approach and relate all staff people to the profitability of the stores they were to help. In many cases, the objectives for the individual central staff people were then the same as the sum of those of the departments in the stores that they helped. At least their objectives would be consistent with those of store departments because the two should be working together to contribute to the overall goal of giving the best possible service to customers at a profit.

Merchandisers Must Look beyond
Gross Margins

In order to carry out the new philosophy of getting central staff to concentrate on profitability of the stores, the president first examined the positions of the merchandisers; they had primarily been responsible for pricing and buying merchandise in their particular spheres. Each had been evaluated by the gross margins of the items that he or she purchased—the difference between the sales price and the purchase price. This seemed logical because gross margin was the part of the total profit that each controlled; it seemed consistent with store profitability.

This overemphasis on gross margins by merchandisers is typical of many retail establishments. It seems only logical that central buyers should be concerned only with their gross margins. After all, they do not actually run the stores and, therefore, do not appear to control other costs.

In this case, the merchandiser emphasis on gross profit had not been consistent with overall profitability of the stores. First of all, it had placed no weight on increasing volume. Its primary deficiency, however, had been that it had failed to balance all costs in the store. The true cost of products to be sold in the store should have included the costs of selling and displaying them.

A prime example of this failure had occurred in the produce departments of the stores. The produce merchandiser had found that it had been more economical to buy produce in large amounts, send it to the central warehouse, and then reship it out in smaller amounts; thus the produce merchandiser had been able to get a better price. Frequently, when the produce had finally arrived at the store, it had required a considerable amount of time by store personnel to clean it up and display it. The cost of this time had not been applied when computing gross margins.

In addition, the produce had frequently not been as fresh as it might have been; the reputation of a store is often strongly affected by the freshness of its produce. In some cases stores could have purchased produce, like fresh corn, cheaper from a local farmer; they could have had it delivered fresh, right off the field. The central produce merchandiser had not permitted them to do this, however. As a consequence, the fresh vegetables delivered from the central warehouse had not been up to the quality of the produce in competitive stores that bought locally.

As the president examined more deeply, he discovered that the merchandisers had not been accountable for outs in the stores. An "out" meant that there had been no merchandise of a particular type available for a customer. Merchandisers had felt that store inventory had been the job of the store manager. The merchandisers had been partially accountable for outs in the central warehouse, however. They had also been accountable for keeping inventory in the warehouse to a minimum.

As the president analyzed this arrangement, he discovered that an out in the warehouse had been considered an out no matter how many stores were affected, no matter what the product was and no matter how many days it was out. In other words, if a major item had been out and affected twenty stores for five days, it had been counted as one out; a minor item that had been out only one day, and affected only one store, had also been considered one out. On the surface it had often appeared as if the outs in the warehouse had not been presenting a serious problem. At the same time store managers had been complaining about a lack of a product to sell.

In addition, stores had often had trouble getting merchandise, particularly special inventory. If a store happened to be in an area of a particular ethnic group that demanded special kinds of merchandise, the merchandiser had not been inclined to buy it because it would have been troublesome to buy in small amounts. Besides, he had felt that gross margins might have been reduced. As a consequence, particular stores had lost some of the ethnic sales potential in their areas.

The president then decided to change the whole merchandiser accountability system and put merchandisers on a basis of net profit in the departments of the stores that they served. They were then in tune with the objectives of the stores. They had to emphasize the volume achieved, the cost of product, and the cost of preparation and merchandising in the stores. An out in any store affected them in that customers would then not purchase the item because it was not available. On the other hand, they were still accountable for the inventory investment in the warehouse. They were accountable, in a balanced way, for the total achievement of the product lines that they purchased.

Specialists Should Improve Store Results

I mentioned earlier that the specialists no longer supervised the departments of the stores that they affected; they were changed from inspectors to helpers of the department managers of the stores. Their big job was the training of store department managers to merchandise better and to train their employees. The specialists' job was defined with a more limited area of influence. They did not directly control the departments of the stores or the people in them. The specialists were now advisors; their specialized know-how was expected to carry weight, but to do so, it had to fit each store's problems. In tune with this philosophy the specialists had to be made accountable for the net profit the stores achieved from the departments they affected. In other words, each one should upgrade the operation of an assigned department of the stores to produce a better profit.

It seemed logical to the president that the specialists should report to the merchandisers who bought and controlled inventory. The merchandisers, too, were accountable for store profit for the departments they served. These two services to the departments of the stores were thereby tied together. In addition, the specialists could give feedback on store problems to the merchandisers to help them control inventory and develop effective merchandising support.

Previously, when a new store had been established, staffing had generally been done by the specialists. Other store managers had often tried to dump their poor performers onto the new stores. The manager of the new store was not sure of this crew and did not have the authority to affect the staffing. As a consequence, many new stores had not taken off the way that they should have.

The president then changed this staffing system and placed the responsibility with the new store managers. It was up to the specialist group to help them get a good staff to get a new store going. They were aiding the store manager instead of controlling the procedure.

The advertising department was like the specialists, a service to the stores, although not necessarily to just one particular department. Their natural tendency had been to develop standard advertising for the total system; it had been cheaper that way and had seemed logical. However, the advertising had frequently not applied to a particular store's local clientele or to local problems caused by competition. The advertising, therefore, had not had maximum sales impact. The advertising director had been further removed from the stores because he had reported directly to the president since the president had been personally interested in advertising.

The president then changed the position of the advertising director and placed him directly under the director of merchandising, who then had control of all the staff services that were supposed to help the stores do a better job of merchandising. The advertising director, in turn, was judged by the sales success of his work. He was then much more inclined to be sensitive to the individual different needs of stores and, thus, part of the central merchandising assistance to the stores.

ORGANIZE FOR STORE EFFECTIVENESS

As the analysis developed a new perspective, the president noticed that new functions had often been added that the chain's increasing size seemed to have made practical. Because of his great interest in these new functions, they had often reported to the president; their importance had loomed large at the time that they were set up. As a consequence, the overall organization plan of the corporation had not kept pace with its growth.

Delegate Functions to Other Executives

The obvious result of adding these functions to those already reporting to the president was that he had too many people reporting to him. Decisions had become more cumbersome. It had seemed natural to have new important functions report to the president. He had been interested in these functions, they had seemed critical at the time, and he had wanted to learn more about them.

The objective, of course, was excellent, but because so many functions had reported to the president, problems had not been handled as quickly as they might have been; decision making had become more cumbersome. In many cases minor problems had been brought to the president; he had wanted to control them and had encouraged this practice. Each item had seemed to involve a substantial expenditure compared to the size of expenditures when the chain had been just a one-store operation. In addition, as the firm had grown, many management people had been placed on new jobs; he had questioned whether he could rely on them to make decisions. This feeling had further bolstered the apparent need to have more decisions come to him.

The president decided to change this whole management approach and rely more on other executives to utilize the new functions. He carefully screened the functions that reported to him to see whether they might be delegated to other executives. One was the advertising director mentioned above.

Another function that had been added had been the bakery. It had been looked at as a critical sales stimulator because the reputation of a store could have been enhanced by its bakery goods. The president had, therefore, wanted to be close to the function.

On analyzing the bakery function, it now appeared to be like any other major department in a store. But it was important to the overall success of the store. He, therefore, placed it under the general merchandise manager.

The central warehouse and transportation department had been set up under a superintendent reporting to the president. Since this function had accounted for considerable expense, the president had wanted to make sure it operated efficiently. As he viewed its function now, however, it also seemed closely related to merchandising; it provided a service to the stores by delivering merchandise when the stores needed it. It was an aid in getting better store results and was important to the success of the merchandisers. He, therefore, had the warehouse and transportation superintendent also report directly to the general merchandise manager. The warehouse and transportation superintendent, too, was then part of the overall central merchandising team and, as such, could be better geared to serve the individual stores.

Provide for Expansion

The firm had grown rapidly and the president was committed to more growth. He now analyzed the company more carefully from this point of view. He noted that new stores had been supervised by the director of operations who had also supervised the ongoing stores. This arrangement had seemed perfectly natural since, eventually, the director of operations would be running these stores. New stores had taken a great deal of time to get going properly; it had been hard for the director of operations to give them the needed attention. As a consequence, the problems of new stores had not been fully met even though the new-store development was critical to the long-term objectives of the firm.

The president decided to set up all new-store development under a director of expansion who was supposed to do whatever was necessary to assure the initial success of the new stores.

In addition, timing had been a problem in starting a new store —dovetailing all details toward a successful opening date. It was also the job of the director of expansion to blend all the work of a store opening toward this date. In a sense, it was a sort of turnkey operation. He should get the new stores going and, when they were going well, turn them over to the director of operations. In order to ensure smooth continuity, the permanent store manager was put in the new store as it got under way.

Because all the new-store operation was placed under the director of expansion, he could more easily tie in with the construction manager and with the manager of sites. In addition, he could coordinate all the start-up to turn over a smoothly operating store to the director of operations. He would spend the time that was necessary to coordinate all the phases of new-store start-up and to expedite them.

A major problem of the new stores had been the training of the permanent employees. In order that training would be done well, a training director was established under the director of expansion. It was the training director's job to make sure that store personnel were fully trained to give good service on the date that the new store opened. It takes time and skill to get all new people up to par. The training director was responsible for developing the methods and approaches needed to train all personnel quickly.

In the past when a new store had been opened, a staff specialist for each department had been sent down into the store for several weeks to help the permanent department manager get it going. In general, the specialist had assisted the department in anything that had to be done but had not taken the responsibility for truly running the department. Nor had the department manager taken this responsibility, because the specialist, the expert, had been there. Neither had taken full responsibility to train the department personnel. As a consequence, it had often taken six to eight weeks to get a new store up to expected service. New stores had been opened up with a great deal of fanfare with special prices to get as many people in the neighborhood as possible to come in initially to shop. Many employees had not been well trained and had therefore given poor service; the new stores often developed a poor reputation at the opening.

The president decided to change the responsibilities in a new store. When a new store was opened, specialists for each department were put into the store as before, but each was temporarily given half the crew of the department to supervise and train directly. The other half of the crew was directly assigned to the permanent department manager, who had been thoroughly trained in how to train the crew. Each had the obligation to train and upgrade the people assigned to him or her so that they could immediately give good service. Both were accountable for the effective launching of the department. After the department was operating smoothly, the specialist was pulled out. This change reduced the time required to get a new store up to speed to about two weeks.

MERCHANDISING IS A BUSINESS

This analysis pointed out that merchandising is a business. In order to get maximum ROM, all the people in a business must be directed toward the overall objective of the business, not just to a segment of the work. In this case, the analysis highlighted the need to change from a staff-dominated operation to one controlled by store managers who were aided by central staff.

It was necessary to tie in every function of the business to help the stores achieve a balanced service at a cost and, as a consequence, produce a profit. As the firm grew, it was especially important to resist the tendency to separate the accountability of the central staff functions from that of the stores. In a sense, they had to be viewed as all being in the same boat together, focusing on the customer.

The store managers were upgraded to assume full responsibility for their stores and, thereby, make the stores effective. Their whole accountability system was changed to emphasize profit and volume, so that objectives reflected the individual conditions faced by each store.

The central staff people were geared to help individual stores after store objectives were individualized; central staff people then changed what they were doing so that their expertise would be utilized in light of the specific, unique requirements of each individual store. Experts were then utilized, not as an overall blanket to cover all operations uniformly, but as a help to each individual store to better serve its customers. The direction of all the functions finally emphasized the individual customer served.

While specialists continued to work with the stores, the emphasis was now on helping, not on supervising. While merchandisers continued to buy and price merchandise, the new direction broadened them to better help the stores overall. In other words, they, too, were brought into balance.

CHAPTER 12

Improving a Complex Operation

Management is presented with a special challenge when trying to analyze a complex, interwoven operation to coordinate it better for higher ROM. There are many more areas where people depend on each other to get the best results. Ever-greater emphasis is required on blending the efforts of management people for maximum results. The job of getting high return throughout the operation becomes more difficult because of the various impacts of different people on the same results.

This challenge presented by the requirement to synthesize diverse work was especially evident in a large petrochemical plant. It consisted of twelve separate units. Each had been turning out its own final products as well as materials for other units. The operation had been made complicated by a constant interflow of product back and forth among the units. The complexity of the operation had been further increased because the final product mix required from the plant had been constantly changing, sometimes daily, depending on the rapidly changing market needs. Since different products had different values per barrel, optimum profitable production and, therefore, optimum product mix could have been quite different at any one time from that of another.

Good comparative data had been available on the industry, and this plant had ranked very favorably both in efficiency and in yield compared to other similar plants. In spite of this good record the vice president of manufacturing was interested in improving the operation still further, however. The overall objective in a deeper management analysis was to get better yields and to lower average costs. In many cases the same factors affected both of these.

INTEGRATE FOR HIGHER PRODUCTIVITY

To some extent, yield had been subordinated to cost because cost data was available in detail. Further, the constant changes in product mix required made it extremely difficult to develop reliable comparative data on yields; the products required and their value had been quite variable. Cost had been controlled by a rather comprehensive expense budget for each part of the operation. This emphasis on cost had not focused on costs in a balanced way, however; the approach had highlighted expenses, not the cost of losses in yield. In many cases a 1 percent loss in yield could have far overshadowed any other cost because of the high volume of product that had been processed in the plant.

The reason for the heavy emphasis on operating costs alone was that the daily product mix had been set by the headquarters scheduling group because of the changing product requirement of the market and because of the tie-in of production with other plants. At times, certain products could have been produced more profitably in other plants of the company. It had been assumed, therefore, that the local plant people could do little to improve yields further—a common misassumption when a firm has central planning and scheduling. The assumption had been strengthened by the fact that yields in this plant had been among the best compared to similar plants in the country.

Measure Yield To Improve It

The main reason that improved yield had not been highlighted in the plant was the difficulty in getting any kind of comparative measurement of yield at all because of the frequent changes in product requirements. Some attempts to measure changes in yield had been made in the past, but it had seemed like combining apples with oranges and cherries; product requirements had changed daily and weekly, and yield potential had changed accordingly. In addition, the expected value of the output from a barrel of crude input could have varied considerably, so the potential value of output was constantly changing. Beyond this, off-quality production in one unit often would have affected yield in another unit. The problem had been compounded by the fact that input and output weights had not been reconciled even over an extended period of time. Because of the strong feeling that the home office controlled yields anyway, improving these measurements had not seemed worthwhile. This conclusion did not prove to be valid when a different approach was taken to the measurement of yields.

The vice president of manufacturing decided that a long-term (one-year) way to measure yield improvements in this interrelated operation must first be developed, even though output and individual product requirements were constantly changing. A cumulative type of measurement of yield was necessary to encourage plant supervision to improve yields further. A satisfactory way was finally worked out by first measuring actual yields compared to targeted yields expected of each unit in each short period of time as set up by the central scheduling department. Targeted yields were then converted to optimum dollar value of the product expected at any one time. These values for short periods were then accumulated to get yearly objectives of the optimum value of product to be produced. The optimum yields were based on the stated product mix needed at the time as determined by the home-office scheduling department. Operating yields actually realized were then also converted to market dollar value at the time of production and compared to targeted value expected. The values of actual yields and of targeted yields for short periods were then added up respectively to get value produced versus optimum value expected for the year. Supervisors then had annual targets plus current data with which they could evaluate how well they were doing against these targets even with the frequent changes in product requirements. Although they were working against daily targets as a control, they were actually measured by annual targets.

The expected product values for each unit were then programmed into a computer so that plant supervision had a continual measurement of performance in terms of optimum dollar accomplishment. In addition, machine operators could check their current operation versus the optimum and make prompt corrections in operating their equipment to get best yield performance. As an incidental, improving the yield improved the cost per unit because operating costs remained the same but output was greater from the same cost. People down the line immediately recognized the appropriateness of the measurement and developed a commitment to control the operation instead of blaming the central office for lack of accomplishment.

It is a common error in complex operations to insist on simplistic measurements that do not fit the operation. A complex operation cannot be simplified by the application of simple measurements. A complex operation usually requires complex measurement to maximize ROM. Whether the operation is complex or not, measurements should encourage the best grass-roots decisions on the problems faced; they should measure real-life problems.

Supervise for Improvement

But the new measurements, in turn, could not be effective unless plant management, all the way down the line, could operate in tune with them. Because it had been assumed that much of the decision making on yield, the major plant achievement, had to be done in the home office, plant supervision had been downgraded; the plant had felt that it should simply follow the master schedule. There had been little local emphasis on training and follow-up of operators by foremen in order to maximize local results, including yield.

It is a common error to deemphasize local supervision when substantial control is centralized and is assumed to be out of the hands of local supervision. This approach leads to less return in any kind of operation.

One evidence of the downgrading of supervision was the practice that had been followed when shifts changed. The plant was a twenty-four-hour operation. The operators, the crews themselves, had rotated shifts in a different way from the way the supervisors and chief operators rotated. As a consequence operators had been assigned to different supervisors and different chief operators each time they rotated. Why? It had been assumed that as long as each shift had the required complement of supervisors and chief operators, the crew had adequate supervision. Presumably, each supervisor or chief operator could have picked up where another left off. Essentially, they had been looking at supervisors, chief operators, and operators as units; they could be plugged in and out at will and still maintain maximum efficiency. Another reason for the rotation was that management had felt that it was good practice to expose operators to several different supervisors and chiefs—the operators would learn more. The consequent lack of commitment of the supervisors and of the chief operators for the training and for the consistent directing of the crews had been ignored.

This rationalization is common in companies with changing supervision, whether it is in a plant, in a sales force, or in a technical project. The practice of frequent changing of supervision almost always leads to poor management, lower ROM, and, strangely enough, poor (not better) training. Exposure to supervisors or practices is not necessarily the same thing as good supervision or training. Supervisors must feel a continuing commitment to maximize the productivity of their subordinates.

The plant manager of this plant then tried to get supervisors and chief operators to rotate with their crews so that they could control the training and supervision and be part of the crew team. An obstacle developed to having supervisors and chief operators rotate with their crews; the wording of the labor contract apparently would not permit it. After careful study, however, it was found that the contract could be interpreted to allow 85 to 90 percent of the crew to rotate with the same supervision. Most of the problem could, therefore, be covered in this way without extensive contract negotiations.

Management often jumps to a quick conclusion that a contract clause is a complete stopper to some management action; in many cases, it is not. If a little ingenuity is applied, a method can be applied to solve much of the problem. There are often ways to approximate good setups even though the labor contract apparently forbids one. In this case, 90 percent of the loaf was far better than no loaf at all.

Lead People Are Not Supervisors

But there was a deeper problem in supervision affecting yield that had to be analyzed. The direct supervising of the employees had been presumably done by the chief operators who were union members; they had been in direct charge of the operators and had been relied upon to teach and supervise the operators. Since the chief operators, themselves, had been hourly people and could also have worked at the equipment under the union contract, this arrangement had seemed to give low-cost supervision. These chief operators had not taken full responsibility for first-line supervision, however; they had not trained operators completely, and they had not been made accountable for the accomplishment of those they directed. Consequently, the chief operator program had actually been high in cost. The losses in costs and yield that had resulted were much greater than the apparent gains by the reduction in supervisory cost. Even the supposed gains in supervisory costs were questionable because, in practice, these chief operators did very little operator work.

The plant manager gradually replaced the chief operators in this plant with full-time supervision. As we mentioned earlier, the plant manager also changed the crew assignment so that supervisors rotated with their crews. These full-time regular supervisors were made accountable for the total accomplishment of their crews—costs, yields, and necessary cooperation with the other units—their crews were their responsibility. The new full-time supervision improved both yield and costs, especially so because the interrelationship between the departments in a complex, interwoven operation like that of this plant was a critical factor for effective operation. The interflows of product between departments required careful attention in all departments all the time.

In any operation supervision (and, as a consequence, productivity) usually suffers when it is carried on by lead people—senior salespeople, senior operators, senior engineers, or senior clerks. Lead supervision gives an illusion of low-cost supervision; it appears as if you are getting supervision from workers. Training and day-to-day supervision suffer, however. There is usually inadequate follow-up because the lead people are not accountable for the maximum productivity of the people they direct. They are not committed to the continued high productivity of their people.

Get Technical Service Close to Operating Problems

Because this operation was highly technical, a central technical service department had been established to give technical service to the twelve operating units of the plant. Both yield and cost could have been affected by the technical advice received by operating supervision. The technical service department had consisted of a technical manager who had supervised twelve technical service engineers and three senior engineers called "senior coordinators." The technical manager had given assignments to the senior coordinators, who, in turn, had given assignments to the technical service engineers. Four technical service engineers had been assigned to each senior coordinator. The senior coordinators had supposedly trained and supervised the technical service engineers; they were not the line supervisors of the technical service engineers, however.

In practice the senior coordinators had received requests to solve technical problems from the various unit superintendents. Generally, the senior coordinators had personally tried to solve all the problems using the technical service engineers as assistants to get information in a so-called legwork capacity rather than letting them take full responsibility for solving the problems. As a consequence, the technical service engineers had not developed into skilled engineers as rapidly as they should have. They had, therefore, been underutilized, and their morale had been low. At the same time, long-range process development that might have improved several units in the plant had lagged. The senior coordinators had not had enough time for plantwide problems; they had been too busy solving current unit problems that had always been occurring.

The plant manager then changed the organization setup so the technical service engineers were assigned to the individual operating units as part of a management module consisting of three operating units; they were then part of an area superintendent's team and were expected to solve technical problems of the units in the module. The area superintendents of the modules were all engineers anyway, and in addition, they had a good knowledge of operating problems so that they could supervise and train the technical service engineers on a functional basis in upgrading them and in providing help to the units on difficult technical problems.

Beyond this, the principal attention of the senior coordinators was directed toward solving larger plantwide problems. They now accomplished more on these big problems than they did before because they were not as involved in day-to-day technical problems. The technical service engineers, who were assigned to the individual units, were now given personal technical projects and, as a result, got much more engineering work done; they did not simply do leg work. Not only did they handle total projects, but they were close to the operating supervisors who would carry out their project plans. The plans were carried through into operation more smoothly. Morale improved substantially.

MINIMIZE DELAYS AND SHUTDOWNS

Dovetailing maintenance with production had been an especially difficult problem in a complex plant operation. Downtime of expensive equipment had been costly. In addition, because of the interflow of product between units, the shutdown of one unit affected the production of other units. Maintenance had to be done well. Although maintenance costs had been quite high, there still had been a great deal of time lost in production because of maintenance shutdowns. The analysis had to be extended into this problem more deeply.

Assign Projects for Completion

All the maintenance work of the plant had been centralized under a maintenance department directed by a general maintenance manager. Under this arrangement the crews had then been assigned easily to any unit where a maintenance problem occurred. Maintenance craftspeople in the maintenance department had been assigned to projects in the operating departments on a daily basis. The assignments had been based on the decision as to which craftspeople had been best-skilled in what had to be done that day in the units. Under this system craftspeople had often been reassigned on the second day of a project, even though the original assignment had not been completed. The new craftsperson assigned to the unfinished assignment had to reanalyze the problem and then carry on with the work.

Here, too, people had been looked at as units; there had been a tacit assumption underlying the system that one maintenance person could be plugged in for another at any point in a project without any loss in effectiveness. After all, they were all skilled craftspeople. However, it had not worked out that way. The replacement craftsperson often reordered parts that the original craftsperson had already ordered; duplicate deliveries to the job site became a common problem because maintenance people had ordered twice. The extra parts had seldom been returned and generally had deteriorated or disappeared; at times, they wound up being carried away by the scrap hauler. In addition, time was lost in completing the projects waiting for the newly ordered parts.

With this daily assignment approach for maintenance craftspeople, different people had often been assigned to the same unit on succeeding problems. They had, therefore, often been unfamiliar with the equipment and, in addition, had not assumed the ongoing responsibility for the continuous smooth operation of the equipment; they only assumed responsibility for fixing a problem to which they had been assigned. The system had not encouraged preventive maintenance work in the first place to prevent shutdowns; the lack of preventive maintenance had, therefore, increased shutdown time. The overall philosophy of the maintenance department had been to concentrate on major shutdowns when they had occurred, not to prevent or minimize them in the first place.

Because all the maintenance work of the plant had been centralized in the maintenance department, craftspeople had been asked to show up for work each morning at the central maintenance office for assignment. It had seemed natural that they should report to their home base to check in. They had then been driven to the location to which they had been assigned for the day; the operating units were spread out over several acres. They had been driven back for their midmorning break and then driven back again to their workplace. They had been driven to the central maintenance office for lunch and back to their jobs again after lunch. The maintenance office had been looked at as their home base from which they had been assigned—that had been where their supervisors had been. Overall, a great deal of time had been spent by craftspeople going to and from the maintenance office to their places of work and waiting for the truck to transport them.

Major Shutdowns Are like Regular Maintenance

Even on major shutdowns, foremen had not had craftspeople regularly assigned to them. The craftspeople had been assigned for each project, and these assignments had also been planned centrally as described above. On this basis the craftspeople had often been assigned to unfamiliar units on shutdowns too. Beyond this, there had been an underlying assumption that a large crew should be assigned to a shutdown of a unit to cover the unit completely; there had been an assumption that the shutdown time would have thereby been minimized, and after all, machine downtime was expensive. The crew size for a particular shutdown had, therefore, frequently been greater than was needed for the work to be done. In addition, because there had been more people in the crew than had actually been needed, they had often gotten into each other's way and thereby reduced productivity. Because several individual members of the large crew had worked on the same parts of the equipment, it had also been hard to establish accountability for specific parts of the shutdown job; in a sense, everybody worked on everything.

Further, regular maintenance and shutdown maintenance had not been tied together even though both had been done on the same equipment with the ostensible purpose of maximizing machine running time. They had been looked at as independent phenomena even though the work done on one should have minimized the work required on the other. Shutdowns had been under the supervision of the foremen of the shutdown crews and, in theory, were supposed to replace much of the preventive maintenance. This approach had seemed sound because the units were twenty-four-hour continuous-process operations; it had seemed too expensive to stop machines for minor repairs. Neither the regular maintenance department nor the operating departments, therefore, took the responsibility for preventive maintenance. Because of this reliance on shutdowns for the maintenance of equipment, operating supervisors had not felt responsible for maintenance cost, even though maintenance cost had been eventually charged against the operating unit; it had seemed logical since they had not supervised the shutdown work.

Make Maintenance a Line Problem

In order to gear maintenance work to operations in a better way, the plant manager then assigned to area superintendents their own maintenance crews; in addition, the crews were housed in the area of the operating units served so that they would be more available to their units. Each area superintendent now managed three operating units and had an area general foreman–maintenance in charge of area maintenance; an area maintenance foreman on each shift had a balanced crew of machinists, painters, pipe fitters, millwrights, and so on to cover regular maintenance in the area. These foremen, in turn, were assigned a permanent crew of craftspeople. At first it seemed impossible to have the area maintenance foreman supervise electronics and electrical work as well as the other crafts, so this work remained in central maintenance, which was tied in by joint accountability for shutdown time caused by electronics or electrical problems.

To make the new arrangement work well, all the area maintenance foremen had to be trained in all the crafts that they supervised; it is hard for any maintenance foreman who is only passingly familiar with the crafts at hand to train people, to lay out jobs, and to make sure that the work is done well; in other words, such a person has trouble getting high productivity from the crew.

The plant manager also changed the responsibility for shutdown time caused by equipment problems; each area general foreman–maintenance of the module (three operating units) was given the responsibility for all shutdowns of the units he or she served. All the people assigned to help in the shutdown were assigned to the general foremen–maintenance of the area concerned, who was made accountable for both shutdown time (including major shutdowns) and current maintenance work (including preventive maintenance work). Under this assignment all maintenance work for an area was under the control of the area general foreman–maintenance.

A central pool of maintenance people was set up in central maintenance, however, so that maintenance foremen of an area could get extra people temporarily or dump an excess as their needs required. They could then keep a lean crew and still take care of bulges in maintenance work. The system worked well because the bulges in the maintenance requirement of the different units did not all occur at the same time.

Under the new organization plan most of the important maintenance work was now directed right in the individual area modules under the control of the area general foreman–maintenance. The best foremen and general foremen were, therefore, assigned to the individual modules; that was where the major potential contribution from maintenance was.

This approach of assigning the best foremen to the operating module is at odds with that taken in many plants where they put the best people in the central departments. In this case, as in many, the main problems to be solved affected first-level operations; staff help should be set up to provide the best assistance to line operations. They can usually do this best if they are close to the problems solved and made accountable for solutions that help the line.

Maintenance Engineering Is Also a Line Problem

Maintenance engineering had been carried out by a plant maintenance engineering department. It had seemed logical that better professional engineering work on maintenance would result if maintenance were centralized in a plant department under a skilled maintenance engineering manager. Presumably, this central group would also provide flexibility in meeting maintenance engineering problems as they arose.

Maintenance engineering had served all the units; individual maintenance engineers had often been assigned to projects in different units in succession. They had not been made accountable for their effect on each individual unit, however.

The plant manager then also decentralized maintenance engineering, and maintenance engineers were assigned directly to the area general foremen–maintenance as part of the area maintenance module. The whole maintenance operation was, therefore, tied together in the module. It was part of the team under the area superintendent.

Maintenance Is both a Line and a Staff Job

As we stated earlier, the operating superintendents had not been fully accountable for maintenance before. That was considered to be the job of the maintenance department. To make the new maintenance organization work well, the plant manager then made the area superintendents accountable for total yield and for total cost; this included the effect of all maintenance, including any cost or loss of yield due to shutdowns. In effect, they supervised their areas almost as if they were complete plants. They were, therefore, accountable for a balance of shutdown costs versus operating costs and yields. To maximize cooperation with the central maintenance department, the central maintenance manager was also made accountable for a balance of maintenance costs and effective running time and was, therefore, encouraged to give help to the operating modules to get better operating results.

An interesting point developed in that slowed-down operation, or "limping," had not formerly been included in shutdown time. Limping meant that the equipment was able to operate but not at full speed. The plant manager had the plant accountant change this measurement so that limping was included in shutdown time; thus when equipment had to operate at 70 or 80 percent capacity, in effect, it was counted as 30 or 20 percent shutdown.

In their reporting many operations make the mistake of not looking at limping production as partial shutdown. In order to get corrective action, anything less than 100 percent operation should be looked at as a delay or a partial shutdown, at least when there is a sufficient backlog of orders to run steadily.

Plan the Shutdown

Previously, shutdowns of units for major overhauls had not been carefully planned in detail; this lack had created a special efficiency problem during shutdowns because of the many interrelated tasks that had to be carried out. Shutdowns of individual units had been generally planned by the central maintenance department in cooperation with the operating superintendent of the department shut down. Between them they had usually decided *what* would be done, but not necessarily *how* in detail.

To correct this shutdown planning problem, a planning manager was set up to plan all shutdowns carefully. The position had the responsibility for planning all materials needed, for purchasing all materials required, for securing all equipment needed, for planning work force and work assignments required, for supervising data processing required, for working out schedules needed, and for satisfying any other requirements of major shutdowns. In order to make sure that the plans were carried through expeditiously, the person was given a planning supervisor, who was accountable for meeting schedules, for meeting projected costs, and for achieving expected performance from maintenance crews during shutdown.

Inventory Is for Use

The plant had also experienced additional delays and maintenance costs because of the way that maintenance materials had been purchased and stored. A great deal of pressure had been applied by the home office to keep inventories low in order to conserve capital. The emphasis had seemed logical because money had been costly. The inventory manager had naturally wanted to meet this pressure. One way that this had been done was by letting some suppliers keep inventory in their own warehouses. Then, when it was needed, the inventory manager had the maintenance material picked up from the supplier warehouses, which were in a major city only 60 miles away. In this way the inventory manager used the supplier inventory instead of increasing the plant's; the procedure allowed the manager to keep in tune with home-office inventory policy.

The idea was superficially sound; in practice, however, when the maintenance crew had wanted a part while doing a repair job, it had often not been in inventory. The inventory manager had secured it immediately, however, by dispatching a pickup truck to the supplier warehouse to get the part and bring it back (a three-hour trip). The maintenance people and the machines had frequently been idle during that period; the extra downtime on the machines had been costly in terms of lost production. Rather than being held accountable for the cost of these delays, however, the inventory manager had looked very good to the home office because of the same low inventory level that had actually caused the delay.

In addition, in order to keep the inventory "clean," the inventory manager had convinced the accountant that inventory costs be charged to the unit as soon as it had been taken out of stock. The inventory manager had not taken the inventory back if it had not been used. No credit had been given to the operating unit if the inventory had been returned; once taken out of stock, it had been operating inventory. On the other hand, the maintenance department had not been truly accountable for the cost of the inventory either. Although the maintenance department checked the parts out of inventory, once a part was taken out of stock, it was charged against the budget of the operating unit where the part was supposed to be used.

The operating units, in turn, had not felt that maintenance cost (including the cost of parts) was theirs either. Even though these costs had been finally charged to them, they had not controlled the maintenance work itself. They had not, therefore, been inclined to do very much about the inventory problem. The whole process had also contributed to additional piles of unused parts inventory in the operating units themselves. Much of it disappeared or deteriorated, and the apparent usage went up.

In addition to pressure on the size of the parts inventory, the inventory manager had home-office pressure on another aspect of the operation—head count (numbers of employees). Since head count had been measured by the number of full-time people, the inventory manager had tried to make up the crew as much as possible by using part-time inventory people. These part-time people had usually been transfers from other departments and had often been temporary. They had not, therefore, been skilled in inventory work; they had been constantly changing and, therefore, been unfamiliar with what was going on in the inventory department; they had not been accountable for the impact on maintenance. The effect had been poor inventory service to the plant coupled with many mistakes; as a consequence mechanics had to wait even longer for parts, so maintenance jobs had been further delayed.

The plant manager then changed the whole inventory operation so that inventory buying, receiving, storage, delivery, and reclaim were all put under one materials manager who was made accountable for the total inventory service, for the delays that the materials department caused in maintenance, and for departmental costs including inventory costs. All the special head-count pressure was taken off; the total cost included payroll costs. It was, therefore, advantageous for the materials manager to have trained, full-time employees to keep costs down. To round out the operation, purchasing was decentralized to the plant to give it more control of the materials that it needed. It, too, was assigned to the materials manager along with inventory. The result was a totally responsible materials department.

Engineering Should Help Operations

Engineering of machinery was another item affecting shutdowns. Central engineering in the home office had been in charge of all major projects; it had been responsible for all the design work (often done by outside consulting design engineers) and, presumably, for the construction resulting from the projects. It had felt a prime obligation for the cost of the equipment that it had designed and built against the estimated cost; the reason for this emphasis was that the cost comparison had been what the executive committee had scrutinized most closely when reviewing engineering projects. Again, like most direct cost data, these figures had always been readily available. Overall, central engineering had not been accountable for performance, maintenance problems, or subsequent yields of the equipment it had designed; these had been looked at as the plant's responsibility. It was central engineering's job to get the equipment in.

This unbalanced accountability is common in many engineering departments. They are not accountable for the net performance of the project afterward, its true purpose. The prime purpose of the project—more effective and low-cost operation—does not carry the same weight as the original cost of the project. It is farther in the future and, of course, affected by the way production people operate the equipment.

In addition, the same engineer in central engineering who had been in charge of a design project had not supervised construction of the equipment itself. Supposedly, the design engineer had been "generally" available for consultation on design during construction, but someone else from central engineering was in charge of it. Further, while there had ordinarily been a plant representative assigned to a project to coordinate with the designers, he or she had not been in on the design work early when the design had been worked out; the project had presumably not been a plant affair until later. By that time the design had been fairly solidified.

The vice president of manufacturing then changed design responsibility so that central engineering was made accountable for the total balanced impact of the unit designed, including the subsequent maintenance costs and yield when it was later in operation. As part of this responsibility, central engineers were expected to write an operating manual for the equipment that would help the production people operate the unit efficiently in order to ensure smooth start-up of the equipment. Their objectives were then in tune with those of the plants. It was further decided that engineers from the plant where the unit was to be built would be assigned to the central engineering project teams early, so that they would be familiar with all the points of design. In addition, they could contribute practical operating knowledge in the design phase in order to forestall subsequent operating or maintenance problems when the equipment was operating. Later, when the unit was built, these engineers were put in charge of construction and were made accountable, with the central design engineers, for subsequent performance of the unit.

COMPLEX OPERATIONS REQUIRE DEEPER FOCUS

What is significant about an analysis of a complex operation? There always seems to be a tendency to oversimplify problems in complex operations. In order to get high ROM from a complex operation, a deeper, more complex analysis is necessary, however. Individual items may have a substantial effect on results, and in a complex operation, there are many more of them than in a simple operation.

The home office could not control the operation. It first appeared as if yield was controlled in the home office. Some aspects of it were. The plant improved it considerably, however, after an unusual measurement was developed to accumulate daily values of production against optimum values. This measurement permitted plant accountability on yields as well as hour-by-hour feedback, so fine adjustments could be made. Operators and foremen could then have an impact on yield.

In order to capitalize fully on the feedback, shifts of supervisors were changed to coincide with those of their crews. Crews became teams with their supervisors. In addition, hourly chief operators were replaced with salaried supervisors in order to make sure that the full job of supervision was carried through.

The plant organization plan was changed to a modular form of organization. Area superintendents were put in charge of three units, to operate essentially like small plants with their own staffs. More operating decisions were then pushed down to the area superintendents.

Each area was given its own technical service engineer reporting to the area superintendent. In addition, it was assigned its own maintenance craftspeople under a general foreman–maintenance to get better tie-ins between maintenance and operations and to reduce shutdown time. In order to encourage total machine control, limping was defined as a shutdown time, and major shutdowns as well as preventive maintenance were then made part of the responsibility of the general foreman–maintenance. A maintenance engineer was also added to the staff of the general foreman–maintenance so that maintenance engineering could be coordinated with the work of the maintenance people of the unit. The general foreman–maintenance, who also reported to the area superintendent, was then given total machine maintenance responsibility in the three units, including responsibility for shutdowns.

Staff was tied in to the module teams. In order to get better control of major maintenance shutdowns, a planning manager was added to plan all the details of materials, equipment, and personnel connected with shutdowns.

In order to prevent waiting time for parts and maintenance supplies, a materials manager position was set up. The materials manager was made accountable for delays caused by lack of materials, for purchasing, for inventory costs, and for his own personnel costs. The head-count emphasis was eliminated so that trained, full-time people were employed in the department.

Central engineering was made accountable for the impact on

plant operation of the equipment it designed, not just for the cost of the equipment. To help it meet this obligation, a plant representative was brought into the design phase early and, in addition, was given major responsibility for the installation of the equipment.

13 Make It Big by Thinking Small

Management problems in all kinds of organizations can be solved, not by broad-brush decisions, but by a careful analytical process of the many small losses that add up to make the big losses. Contrary to popular opinion, there is not ordinarily any one big item, such as a major policy, a major program, or a major influx of money, that will by itself substantially increase ROM.

It is also disappointing to depend on specialized analyses of parts of a problem. The work of each specialist must be blended into a holistic management process and compromised with the work of other specialists to encourage people toward maximum ROM.

In order to realize the big gains, the focus should be on all levels of the organization, not just on the top. This focus would include the bottom management level and, I should say, *especially* the bottom level. After all, that is the place where most actual return from higher managers shows up; that is where their decisions must impact. This approach is the key to management productivity and so to all productivity in an organization.

WHAT CHARACTERIZES ROM

The most promising way to develop this management approach for increasing ROM starts with a philosophy based on people—their feelings and their interests. It should be directed toward what motivates management people and, perhaps more important, what demotivates them. The aim should be one of creating a climate that considers all the pressures on the individual, no matter what his or her position, and attempts to make them strongly positive. In this process it is recognized that people will do what they think is advantageous to them; they will work toward what they think is the best possible blend of the pressures that are being exerted on them.

Analyze the Management Climate

In order to get the best return from their subordinate management people, higher managers and executives must be able to analyze the problems of their subordinates in terms of losses and the difficulties they face in reducing these losses. It is then the prime responsibility of higher managers to set a management climate of strong positive pressures that encourage the higher return they desire. Executive decisions and broad directives are no substitute for creating this management climate. But the development of this climate is a painfully meticulous process and cannot be done by a broad-brush approach.

Make Pressures Positive

The key to improved ROM is then the changing of all pressures on management people to make them strongly positive in the best direction of accomplishment desired from the organization. This would hold true whether the people involved were in a plant, in a sales department, in a technical department, or in an administrative department. In each situation higher executives must be primarily concerned with the management climate being developed all the way down to the bottom level of the organization. That is where their own results finally show up. In practice a major emphasis must be placed on turning what would otherwise be negative pressures on individuals, pressures working against accomplishment, into positive pressures encouraging accomplishment. In other words negative pressures must be neutralized and, if possible, turned into positive pressures.

In analyzing these pressures, executives must consider the effect of any kinds of policies on the total work of people at all levels. These policies could be employee relations policies, sales policies, or manufacturing policies, for example. Procedures almost inevitably follow policies; executives must also be alert to the effect that procedures have in exerting negative pressure against the accomplishment of management people. These restrictive procedures usually develop by the way staff people conscientiously try to carry out an executive's policies. In general, they tend toward overkill because staff people want to make sure that they do not miss any area. Executives must first analyze the effect of this overkill and then restrain it if they are to reduce the negative pressures on people down below.

Some of these negative pressures come from the special emphasis of specialists pushing the influence of their specialties beyond the point where they are productive in coping with the losses. Again, executives must restrain specialists and weave their activity into the overall result that the line is trying to accomplish; they must compromise the work of each specialty.

In any management analysis, recognition systems should be reexamined to see whether they are flexible enough to emphasize the right pressures in every job in light of the specific accomplishment now expected. Organization procedures and plans should also be reviewed on the same basis. It is all too common to look at organization structure on a broad basis instead of as the specific organization plan needed for specific accomplishment in a specific area in a particular period of time. Long-term organization structures need to be constantly reviewed, or they become stumbling blocks to accomplishment.

Budgets and accounting systems must be especially analyzed more deeply to make sure that they are not being applied on such a uniform basis that they become insensitive to the specific requirements of each management job and, therefore, exert pressure against accomplishment. In other words, positive management pressures to be achieved through reports should not be sacrificed for the sake of uniform accounting procedures.

It is, in short, the job of an executive to analyze all the various pressures on people down the line and to make sure that they are positive as they affect drive for accomplishment. To do this, an executive must develop a new understanding of the way all policies, procedures, and systems affect the pressures on people down the line. Specialists in personnel, product management, engineering, cost accounting, and now in the computer field must all be studied from the point of view of their total impact on line people. It is the job of the executive to make sure that they result in positive pressures, positive help to the accomplishment expected of the line. Otherwise, staff frequently pushes line too far in a single, specialized direction, resulting in a negative pressure against some other results that the executive wants the line to get.

Overall, the most important job of any higher manager or executive is to develop an invigorating climate for ROM for each of the management people down the line. It is the best way to meet the objectives set by the executive. It is important that the effect of all policies, procedures, and programs is positive when they finally impinge on the individual. Executives must be constantly on the alert to detect places where a negative impact is being felt by people down the line. Executives must, therefore, be open to complaints from people down the line regarding these negative pressures and not brush them aside as just normal gripes about any procedure. A continuing management analysis is required of the way that people are subjected to these pressures.

Compromise Is the Order
of the Day

The key element in developing this invigorating management climate is the intelligent compromise of all pressures. Any pressure may have a good effect but only up to a certain point. It is the sum total of all the pressures that results in the highest ROM. Any one pressure becomes negative when it is pushed too far. Recognition for one result may prevent a management person below from pushing hard for another result where there is little or no recognition. As a case in point, heavy pressure on the engineering costs of an equipment design project may result in less pressure on future maintenance and operating costs and, therefore, in lower ROM from the project. A requirement that a successful marketing approach used on one product under one set of conditions should be used on all products under a variety of conditions must be reexamined in the same light. Does it present obstacles to the success of other products marketed under other conditions?

All procedures and all programs that have been successful must be reanalyzed to point out their weaknesses as they apply to the particular conditions that people are facing today. In other words, management is constantly walking a tightrope; it is trying to balance the various influences to get the optimum push in the right direction. It should not be unduly swayed by any one specialist or by any one successful procedure but put them all into perspective.

To make these compromises properly, "generalist" executives must know the values and limitations of specialists. In addition, they must be sensitive to the needs of jobs all the way down the line in order to set the climate there for maximum productivity. Their communications plan must feed up to them the difficulties and the problems that people at all levels are facing trying to maximize their ROM. They must resist the temptation to catalog complaints below as mere grousing—"They just don't see the total picture."

The continuing use of the four-step analytical process for management makes management better able to adjust to change, a critical factor in these days of constant change. It is inherent in this process that managers are constantly analyzing losses that are occurring *today*. The process automatically makes them more sensitive to changed conditions that, in turn, require changes in management pressures in order to maximize the ROM of their people today.

USE THE FOUR-STEP ANALYSIS TO INCREASE ROM

Managers can best meet the problems of increasing ROM by the four-step analytical process we have developed throughout this book. It is a process whereby a manager can effectively analyze those factors that are antagonistic to ROM in the management jobs below and take constructive action to neutralize them.

Define the Loss

As we have seen in the examples described in previous chapters, in the first instance the emphasis in such an analysis should be placed on what accomplishment management people at different levels are losing or what additional accomplishment they might achieve. In other words, what are the losses that might be prevented or what are the additional potential gains that might be obtained in each particular management job? Each of these losses or gains should be measurable in terms of the goals of the institution. For example, they could be defined as less yield, higher personnel costs, less profitable sales, or profit return when a new product is launched; they should not be word descriptions of a bad situation.

On the other hand, it may be true that morale or past attitude is a problem; however, this is difficult to correct when described in that way. Lack of consumer acceptance may be a problem, but it is not easily approached in a practical sense from that definition. Higher technical excellence of a product design may seem to be a good description of an objective, but it is difficult to attack managementwise unless carried further to a loss or a potential gain. Until the description of a bad situation is carried to a measurable loss or a potential gain, it is not easily susceptible to sound management analysis.

Even when focusing on a loss, there is a tendency for people to want to describe losses on a broad overall basis—total decline in sales, broad increase in costs, etc. In practice each of these losses must be broken down into smaller and smaller losses if they are to be intelligently attacked. This is the key to getting higher ROM from management people down the line.

For example, it may not be true that you have an overall reduction in sales of 10 percent. It is hard to come to grips with a broad loss of this type, however. On the other hand, if you are able to state that there is a 15 percent decline in x product sales in the New England region, the loss may be attackable. If you were to say that there was a 10 percent higher cost per unit than should be the case in a plant, it may be very difficult to pinpoint answers. But if you break this excessive cost down to describe a 15 percent increase in night-shift unit costs in the machining department, you now have a workable area to attack. At that point you may start to get down to individual management people and lead to the pressures that affect those people when trying to get the cost reduction you want.

In order to get higher productivity all the way down the line, major losses must be divided and redivided to make them manageable and susceptible to sound analysis. Only then can corrective measures be effectively worked out. It should be reitereated that these smaller losses cumulatively make up the big ones, so that in the process of solving the many small losses, you are, in practice, solving the large ones.

As we have seen in previous chapters, many times a loss develops in one result area because undue emphasis was placed on another laudable result; in other words, the problem was one of imbalance. In almost every case, special emphasis on one result will detract from the accomplishment of another result. People have a limited amount of time and energy to apply to problems. What they apply in one area, they cannot apply in another. A management analysis must seek balance or compromise so that emphasis is properly distributed upon all the worthwhile results.

A Loss Has a Direct Cause

The next step in carrying the analysis forward is to determine the specific trigger that directly caused the loss in the first place. It could be a specific physical action, like a chemical reaction; it could be the way a machine operated, like a casting machine. More often it is a specific action of someone, like the late delivery of orders; a machine operator may operate in a certain way that causes problems for other people. As we saw in the cases described in previous chapters, a demand of staff for compliance to what appears to the staff person to be a fine procedure to assure control could cause the loss. A common case is that in which losses occur because of a management failure to demand training of subordinates. Although almost every company says that it emphasizes training, in practice, as we noticed in the cases cited, the actual training of the employees is not required. There is often little money or time set aside in the budget to provide for the training; as a consequence, it is not carried through. Losses may be caused by a practice on the part of a department to treat all problems the same way. For example, a manufacturing department may treat new products or products for the international division the same way as it did old products for U.S. divisions.

In most cases we saw that several causes worked together to trigger a loss or to fail to prevent it. In real life, multiple causes tend to be the rule. For example, yield in one case was affected because of inadequate supervision, but it was also affected by the requirement that product running decisions were made by central scheduling. These factors were added to by limping in production caused by an attempt to reduce maintenance costs. The setup was further weakened by a lack of control of in-process material from a previous department.

Management Action Always Precipitates a Cause

Interestingly, behind every cause we have found some management action that has set the climate which initially precipitates the cause. This action is always action by people higher up in the management chain, by higher management, or by executives. For example, we saw how executive decisions on pay programs or on appraisal plans often forced misdirection. In other cases a requirement for tight budget adherence discouraged creative work for the future and reduced long-term ROM. In still other cases an executive tendency to view dealers and distributors as customers rather than as part of the company marketing team forced company programs onto a track that resulted in less service to final consumers and less profit for the firm. A new-product development group had little concentration on costs because higher management had put heavy emphasis on quality beyond the point where it was needed in the market.

We have come to the conclusion that all lack of ROM in some way traces back to an action of higher management that puts adverse pressure on people below, preventing them from accomplishing as much as they could have. The management action frequently comes from executive decisions, even though the actual pressure occurs through the work done by staff. Central staff, after all, only carries through as a result of executive decision. It tries to satisfy what it understands to be the desires of higher line management.

It is this central staff management action that ordinarily creates most of the pressures as you come down the management chain. It is actually the indirect effect of executive decision, however. Policies, overall programs, and executive decisions result in procedures that exert pressure on people below and misdirect them. It is the main reason for their failure to get high productivity in their jobs. A broad overall policy or an overall program always gets down to specific procedures in application which, in turn, exert pressures on management people below.

As we have seen, there may actually be several management actions that contribute to a cause. For example, several policies might impinge on a management person at any one time, each exerting pressure. Several different procedures or programs may impinge on individuals pushing them off the track. A management analysis must trace each of these and correct it at its source.

Why Was the Management Action Taken?

There is a tendency, particularly in younger people, to jump too quickly to the conclusion that an action that seems to prevent something from being accomplished is stupid. As you could see in the cases we described, this is not true. When you dig deeply enough, you find that there was always a logical reason for the management action that may have caused the problem you see now. People who initiated it were usually intelligent people—experienced people who were doing their best to solve a problem they were facing. They had a problem, and they probably solved it by the very policy or procedure that seems to be causing difficulty now. If you make a change, you want to be sure you do not lose the gain that was once achieved by instituting the policy or procedure in the first place and revert back to the original problem.

However, conditions today may be different from what they were when the policy was instituted. In this situation you may be incurring little risk by changing. But you have to make sure that the loss is thoroughly analyzed in light of today's conditions and, in light of those conditions, that the policy or procedure be changed (to some extent at least) in order to improve ROM today.

At the time the policy or program was instituted, it may have positively affected a particular result. What may not have been envisioned was that it would negatively affect other results. This phenomenon was true in most of the cases that we reviewed. Management problems are very complex and have many tentacles. It is hard to determine a policy or a procedure that will work superbly in one direction and affect nothing else negatively. Other results are affected by the pressures that develop from emphasis on one result. In many cases though, these policies or programs could be changed to some extent and still retain the benefits on the first result that was affected. A compromise solution must be effected.

In this phase of the analysis, management principles are helpful in clarifying the reasons that the management action was taken and perhaps, in addition, clarifying why it should not have been taken. Frequently, the management action may have been approached too simplistically by applying just one management principle. In practice you need a compromise of principle; this compromise of principle is the ultimate key in all management problems. A management principle is best viewed as stating a force; it does not state an absolute cause-result relationship, only an influence. In solving a particular management problem, several principles have to be compromised in order to get the highest ROM from the individuals involved. Principles should only be looked at as aids in the solution of management problems.

Analysis Leads to Solution

If the management analysis has been carried through thoroughly from the loss to the cause, to the management action, and then to the reason for it, the solution is very often apparent. The critical part comes in making the initial four-step analysis. It must go deeply enough. People frequently jump to solutions too quickly instead of doing the hard, meticulous work that is required to follow this four-step analytical process. In our experience it always pays to follow it as we did in the cases reviewed in the previous chapters.

WHAT THE ROM APPROACH DOES

As indicated in the case examples in this book, the four-step analytical approach aims at correcting management problems and thereby increasing ROM. It tries to get away from simply setting the blame for a problem. In some cases blame may be attached in order to get correction by sound management pressure but never simply to set it as such in the hope that correction will automatically ensue.

This analytical approach makes the information flow more positively; it turns away from simple, negative finger pointing and gears an information system to create in a better way positive help and encouragement to the individual management person down the line. The approach is critical for executives in order to use a computer intelligently to aid in applying positive encouragement. Although a computer can be very helpful in applying positive pressure, it is of limited value, however, in thinking out the solutions. Individuals develop and install solutions as a response to the pressures on them; the computers, as developed today, have not arrived at the point where they seem able to do this thinking.

The four-step approach leads to more realistic cooperation and smooth interaction between people who should be cooperating toward results. As organizations become large and more complex, executives experience increasing difficulty in getting the needed cooperation between various management people toward results that the organization wants to achieve; organizations become slow and cumbersome. This analytical process aims at developing a management environment that will encourage sound cooperation instead of discouraging it. Many times, an analysis ferrets out the pressures that discourage people from cooperation; these anticooperation pressures are often the main deterrent to the attainment of high ROM. As a result of this analysis of cooperation, new types of staff expertise that are coming up on the horizon are used more productively; they are more helpfully blended into the current operation, instead of being an accretion that the rest of the organization has to bear and, hopefully, find some way to utilize.

The four-step process develops management people; it encourages all managers to broaden their outlook and become generalists. They learn to utilize specialists more intelligently to eliminate losses, instead of looking at each specialist as independent of the rest of the organization; they consider each specialty from the point of view of its impact on each individual person down the line.

In the process guides are developed so that specialists can fit their expertise into general line problems. In this way specialists are also broadened.

Since a management analysis tries to wind up with the best compromise setup of pressures on management people, it establishes a sound management climate for management development. It encourages managers to learn to analyze realities of pressures that prevent losses. Further, it encourages them to carry through to make sure that these pressures become positive and result in gains in return. Overall, the analytical management process allows management to capitalize on more of the 50 percent of management ability that is usually lost in organization. It aims at unlocking the great potential that exists in the management structure of any organization. It encourages all pressures on management people to be positive, so that each management person becomes a more vibrant, aggressive achiever toward the results the institution wishes to achieve.

Management analyses provide a base for broadening individuals at all levels of management, and as such they are in tune with the social trends developing today toward allowing people to develop fully the potentials of which they are capable. In applying the process, management develops broader citizens because it develops people who are able to think more broadly and look at complex problems more realistically—a critical need for a vital democratic society.

In summary, the four-step ROM analysis gets all managers thinking in terms of the realities of the bottom level of people in the organization and of the smaller problems that make up the bigger ones. Through the process, they then make it big by thinking small.

Index

80709

HOYT

DATE DUE
